F

MW00463763

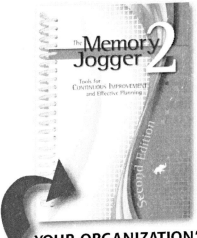

The Memory Jogger 2

Tools for
CONTINUOUS IMPROVEMENT
and Effective Planning

Second Edition

YOUR ORGANIZATION'S
LOGO HERE

To place an order, get a quote, or ask about
this customization promotion contact GOAL/QPC

800.643.4316

603.893.1944 | service@goalqpc.com

Free Customization*

Align your organization with other continuous improvement tools.

Visualize Your Logo Here

While supplies last, minimum quantity order 25.

To place an order, get a quote, or ask about this customization promotion contact GOAL/QPC

800.643.4316

603.893.1944 | service@goalqpc.com

The YELLOW BELT Memory Jogger™

A Guide for the Six Sigma and Lean Six Sigma Team Member

Joseph T. Basala
First Edition / GOAL/QPC

The Yellow Belt Memory Jogger™: A Guide for the Six Sigma and Lean Six Sigma Team Member

Six Sigma is a federally registered trademark of Motorola, Inc.

Development Team:

Author: Joseph T. Basala, *QI Sigma Consulting, Inc.*

Project Management: Daniel Griffiths
                     Susan Griebel

Cover Design and Layout: Michele Kierstead

Graphics: GOAL/QPC staff

Editor: Francine Oddo

Photo credit on page 97: Race car pitstop, Robert Doyle

GOAL/QPC | Memory Jogger
8E Industrial Way, Suite 3, Salem, NH 03079
800.643.4316 or 603.893.1944
service@goalqpc.com
MemoryJogger.org

Printed in the United States of America
ISBN: 978-1-57681-173-3

10 9 8 7 6 5 4 3 2 1

Acknowledgments

I would like to offer my sincerest thanks and gratitude to the following individuals who took time out of their busy schedules to review the draft of *The Yellow Belt Memory Jogger*™ and offered their invaluable advice and suggestions. Certainly, they added value to this book and their contributions were very much appreciated.

Reviewers

Michael D. Jones
P.E., Master Black Belt

Elizabeth M. Keim
Master Black Belt and Managing Partner,
Integrated Quality Resources, LLC

Chad Smith
Master Black Belt and Owner, Continuous
Improvement Solutions, LLC

Mary Beth Soloy
Master Black Belt, Ford Motor Company

How to Use This Pocket Guide

This pocket guide is designed for you to use as a convenient and quick reference guide. The "What is it?" "Why do it?" and "How do I do it?" format offers you an easy way to navigate through the information in each section.

Use this guide as a reference on the job, or during and after your training, or as part of a self-study program. Put your finger on any individual concept, tool, or phase of the DMAIC process within seconds.

Jogger Positions

Getting Ready—When you see the "getting ready" position of the runner, expect a brief description of the step or task, or the purpose of using a tool and its benefits.

Cruising—When you see this runner, expect to find guidelines and interpretation tips. This is the action phase that provides you with step-by-step instructions and helpful formulas.

Finishing the Course—When you see this runner, expect to see the result of a task or step, or a tool in its final form.

DMAIC Model

DMAIC   DMAIC   DMAIC   DMAIC   DMAIC

Look for these icons to begin reading about the steps, tasks, and tools used in that particular phase of the model.

This icon **Advanced DMAIC** indicates tools that Green/Black Belts use that Yellow Belts may find helpful to know about.

Specific Tools for the Yellow Belt

Look for this icon **2 Core Tool** to get details on a tool that a Yellow Belt should understand and know how to use. Use the Quick Tool Finder to find the page number of these tools.

Tips and Pitfalls

When you see **Tip**, you'll get tips on a step or method, or further explanation of a concept.

Look for this icon, ⚠ for ideas on how to avoid many of the common pitfalls associated with the steps and tasks within the phases of the DMAIC model.

Quick Tool Finder

CONTENTS

ABOUT THE AUTHOR

Joseph (Joe) T. Basala

Master Black Belt, QI Sigma Consulting, Inc.

Joe Basala has approximately 25 years of experience in service, manufacturing, and engineering quality. He is focused on the implementation and deployment of Six Sigma/Lean Six Sigma. Joe has provided Lean-Six-Sigma-related training and coaching to individuals from 100+ different companies representing industries such as: beverage, distribution services, banking and finance, aerospace, chemical, automotive, software/IT, and numerous general service and manufacturing organizations.

In a previous role, he served as the Technical Leader (Master Black Belt) for a company's continuous improvement process (Six Sigma). In that assignment, Joe provided technical guidance worldwide to the Champions and Black Belts on topics such as project selection, process methodology, and proper use of the various statistical and quality tools.

Joe has a Bachelor's degree and a Master of Science degree from Western Illinois University and a Master of Business Administration degree from St. Ambrose University.

He is an ASQ Fellow, and also has the following certifications: Certified Six Sigma Master Black Belt, Certified Six Sigma Black Belt, Certified Manager of Quality/Organizational Excellence, Certified Reliability Engineer, Certified Quality Engineer, and Certified Quality Auditor.

Joe is a past Chair of ASQ's Six Sigma Forum Advisory Council. He is also a member of the Editorial Review Board for ASQ's Six Sigma Forum Magazine.

INTRODUCTION

Six Sigma has been a popular process-improvement methodology for more than two decades. It is implemented by selecting and executing process- and product-improvement projects. Project leaders (Green and Black Belts) guide a team through the tools and methodology to enable the team to meet customer requirements.

Much of the training and commonly available literature has historically focused on champions, and Black Belt and Green Belt project leaders. Yellow Belts (team members) are a more recent addition to the Six Sigma infrastructure.

The purpose of *The Yellow Belt Memory Jogger™* is to discuss the tools that Six Sigma team members who have been trained should know. It is becoming more common to train team members as Yellow Belts because of the benefits that they bring to teams and projects.

Yellow Belts, who assist the team leader on a project, contribute skills that facilitate all team members by taking more of an active role in a project. This involvement can accelerate a team's ability to complete projects, and it can extend the reach of the project leader, as team members can handle more project responsibility.

Whether team members find themselves in a Six Sigma or Lean Six Sigma project, they will find the descriptions of the tools presented in this book to be valuable.

The overall objective of this Memory Jogger is to provide Yellow Belts with a reference guide that addresses these types of questions:

- What is Six Sigma?
- What is the DMAIC cycle for process improvement?
- What are the roles within Six Sigma?
- What are the tools that Yellow Belts most need to know? How are these tools used?
- What are some guidelines for interpreting them?
- What tools are commonly used in each phase of the DMAIC cycle?
- What are some tools that Green-level and Black-level Belts use that Yellow Belts might encounter on a project?

A recent trend is to utilize Lean manufacturing tools in addition to Six Sigma tools, which creates a hybrid known as Lean Six Sigma. It is also very common for organizations to create their own names for their continuous improvement methods to facilitate buy-in within the organization. No matter the exact name or spin on the methodology, the Yellow Belt will find knowledge of the tools to be of value.

Lean tools are included in the body of knowledge (BoK) for many Six Sigma training programs and certification models. For simplicity, this book often uses the term Six Sigma to also include the term Lean Six Sigma.

What is Six Sigma?

Six Sigma is a business-improvement methodology with roots tracing back to the Motorola company in the mid-1980s. Specially trained project leaders (called Belts) lead a team to solve problems identified by the business. A combination of proven quality and statistical tools are employed to develop a solution. A problem-solving framework called DMAIC (Define, Measure, Analyze, Improve, and Control) is used to improve existing processes and products.

For the development of new products and processes, a variation of Six Sigma called Design for Six Sigma (DFSS) is used. DFSS is not as standardized as DMAIC, but one common framework is DMADV (Define, Measure, Analyze, Design, and Verify).

There is a great deal of commonality in the tools used in both DMAIC and DMADV. One main difference is in the sequence and rigor of tool usage. This book covers the DMAIC approach.

Sometimes a shorthand term of 6σ or 6 Sigma or 6s is used to represent Six Sigma. Sigma (σ) is a Greek letter used to symbolize the term standard deviation, a unit of measure of variation. While there is some complexity (and confusion) in the measurement of Six Sigma, for discussion purposes it can be said that if a process has six standard deviations (short term) between the mean and the specification limits, it is operating at a Six Sigma level of performance. Given certain assumptions, a Six Sigma process could be expected to have approximately 3.4 defects per million opportunities over the long term (99.99966% defect free).

To illustrate 6σ performance, here's an example:

A bank is interested in yearly teller absenteeism. The bank has 50 branches across the country and each branch employs four tellers. Employees in each branch have an 8-hour workday and 250 working days in the year. If this bank has a 3σ level of performance, then there are 26,724 hours of absenteeism over the course of the year. At 4σ, the absenteeism would be 2,484 hours. If the performance is at 6σ, the bank would experience only 1.4 hours of employee absenteeism.

In the short term, a 6σ process would have an extremely high level of performance as measured by the low number of defects that would be produced.

In the Short Term
Process is Centered

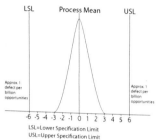

LSL=Lower Specification Limit
USL=Upper Specification Limit

Some companies have found that processes on average experience a degradation in performance over the long term as all the sources of variation have an impact on the process. This degradation can be visualized as a linear shift in the process.

Over the Long Term
Process shifted by 1.5 standard deviations

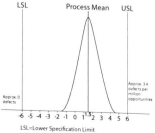

LSL=Lower Specification Limit
USL=Upper Specification Limit

Tip: There is a table in Appendix A that shows the process sigma level, from 0 to 6, the corresponding defects per million opportunities, and the percentage that is defect free (yield). For a deeper understanding of sigma, consult your team's Black Belt, *The Six Sigma Memory Jogger™ II,* or *The Black Belt Memory Jogger™.*

To further illustrate linear shift over the long term, recall the previous example of the bank with 50 branches across the country that wanted to examine yearly teller absenteeism. The example stated the total number of hours that tellers would be absent from the job (performance of the characteristic) at 3, 4, and 6 Sigma levels. These values (for hours absent) represent absenteeism over the course of a year, and reflect the 1.5 linear shift.

The reason is that over time, the bank will experience sources of variation that may not be present in the short term. Circumstances such as tellers staying home with sick children, teller illnesses, alarm clock malfunctions, weather and other traffic delays, transportation breakdowns, etc., may all contribute more variation over time.

If the attendance characteristic is operating at a 6 Sigma level of performance in the short term, it will still have a low defect rate in the long term (about 3.4 defects per million opportunities when all the sources of variation show up).

The concept of "short term" versus "long term" variation can be confusing since it is not really tied to calendar time. To be considered "long term," process data needs to contain most (if not all) of the sources of variation that could exist.

Many companies have found that there is a linear shift of approximately 1.5 standard deviations between short term and long term. The concept of linear shift shows how more defects will be created over the long term, however, in reality the standard deviation will be larger (due to all the sources of variation that will occur), which in turn increases the spread of the output around the process average.

Why use Six Sigma?

Teams that have used a 6σ methodology have demonstrated their ability to generate bottom-line savings and top-line growth for organizations. Six Sigma has helped organizations develop a common methodology and approach within their business to drive continuous improvement.

How is Six Sigma done?

1. Business leaders come to realize that current improvement methods could be improved by adding the structure and skills of 6σ. Often a deployment plan is created, detailing how the organization will go about pursuing Six Sigma.

2. Business leaders identify ideas for potential projects, and a prioritization strategy is used to identify the critical projects.

3. Project leaders and teams are assigned. (Project leaders can be Master Black Belts, Black Belts, or Green Belts.)

4. The project leader and team work through the DMAIC problem-solving methodology.

5. Tollgates, or reviews, are done at defined milestones during the project to make sure the project is on track to deliver the results in sync with business and customer needs.

6. When the project is completed, responsibility for managing the improved process is transitioned back to the process owner. The project leader and team may be assigned to a new project based on the needs of the business.

7. Since project results may not lead to a desired state with one DMAIC cycle, the business problem can again be added to the list of potential projects for prioritization. Also, other project ideas are often discovered by the team during a project and can be added to the list.

How is Six Sigma done?

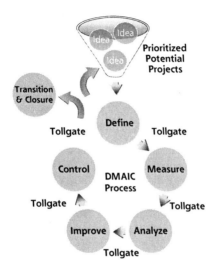

Prioritized Potential Projects

Transition & Closure

Tollgate

Define Tollgate

DMAIC Process

Control Measure

Tollgate Tollgate

Improve Analyze

Tollgate

Tip: It is very helpful for the team to identify a post-project audit plan (described in Chapter 5). This will ensure process controls are maintained and improvements are sustained over time.

DMAIC Model

Define	Measure	Analyze	Improve	Control
Identify Voice of the Customer (VOC)	Create Process Map	Identify Sources of Variation	Develop Solution	Validate Improved Process Capability and Measurement System
Conduct Project Selection	Conduct Measurement Systems Analysis	Use Graphical Analysis for Screening	Mistake Proof Solution	Implement Process Controls
Create Project Charter	Collect Data	Use Statistical Analysis to Identify Critical Inputs (X's)	Pilot Solution	Complete Project Documentation
Assign Team	Calculate Basic Statistics			
Create SIPOC	Calculate Six Sigma Capability Metrics			

The steps in each column have been consolidated, or simplified, for this book. For more details on DMAIC, consult *The Black Belt Memory Jogger™* and *The Six Sigma Memory Jogger™ II*.

Roles and Responsibilities

What are the roles and responsibilities within Six Sigma?

Why use these Six Sigma roles?

These roles provide the needed structure and focus to make projects successful. They are commonly used and proven to work.

How are these roles defined?

- A champion or steering council is appointed to guide the deployment of Six Sigma.

- Criteria are defined for each role.

- A strategy for organizational training is developed and executed.

- Due to the maturity of Six Sigma, many people come into an organization with the appropriate background and knowledge. If individuals—from the executive level to the "hands-on" person doing the work—do not have the appropriate level of knowledge, they should be given training on Six Sigma, and on their roles to achieve it.

Example of Typical Training Requirements

Executive	1 day
Champion	2 + days
Master Black Belt	Black Belt + additional technical and interpersonal skill development
Black Belt	4 weeks
Green Belt	2 weeks
Yellow Belt	**2 days**
Employee or White Belt	4 hours

© 2015 GOAL/QPC

It is also common for individuals and organizations to pursue certification—either internally or through a third party such as the American Society for Quality (ASQ)—to verify that Belts have attained at least the minimum level of knowledge needed for that level of 6σ Belt.

> **Tip:** Each organization needs to consider how these roles should be deployed internally. For example, a service-oriented organization might benefit more from a larger group of Green Belts, while a more technology-driven organization might benefit more from the skill set that Black Belts can offer. A deployment model perfect for one organization might be completely wrong for another organization.

DMAIC Tollgate Reviews

 What is it?

A tollgate review occurs between each phase of a Six Sigma project to ensure that the intent of the project is maintained. Reviews are attended by key individuals like the champion, the Master Black Belt, Black Belts, Green Belts, and key stakeholders.

Why do it?

Tollgate reviews are done to answer questions like:

- Should the project continue?

- Is the project on track?

- What actions need to be done before the project advances?

How do I do it?

1. Set meeting dates in advance as soon as possible to ensure key members can attend.

2. The project leader (Master Black, Black or Green Belt) prepares a project summary to review with the group.

3. Typical questions that are answered during the reviews for each phase are shown on the next two pages.

Define Phase   DMAIC

- Have customers and key stakeholders been considered?
- Has the project been fully chartered?
- Is the team in place?
- Has a project plan been developed?

Measure Phase   DMAIC

- Has the process been fully characterized by including steps, inputs, outputs, cycle times and so on?
- What are the defects or waste in the process?
- Can key variables be adequately measured?
- What is the baseline process capability?

Analyze Phase   DMAIC

- Have all the critical inputs been identified?
- What are the sources of variation and waste?

Improve Phase   DMAIC

- Is the solution feasible?
- Does the solution meet the intent of the charter?
- Is the solution statistically significant?
- Were the results of the pilot appropriate to move forward?
- Is training needed and have new training materials been developed?

Control Phase   DMAIC

- Has the process documentation been updated? This documentation includes the process map, FMEA, policies, procedures, work instructions, the control and audit plans, and a final report.

- Are all the controls in place?

- Is the measurement system still adequate?

- Does the solution meet the amount of improvement required by the charter?

- Is the final report written?

- Have any other projects been identified as a result of this project?

- Can the results of the project be leveraged somewhere else?

- How will the project be closed out?

- Will there be a team celebration?

4. Additional actions that are needed are added to the project plan and executed.

Tip: It is rare for a project to be terminated mid-cycle if the Define phase was thoroughly completed. However, as new information is uncovered during the project, this is a possibility that could develop and should be considered, if necessary.

Chapter 1

DMAIC: Define Phase

Typical Steps

Identify Voice of the Customer (VOC)

Conduct Project Selection

Create Project Charter

Assign Team

Create SIPOC

If this phase is skipped or done superficially, significant issues can result later in the project. Issues like:

- The team tries to solve the wrong problem.

- The team tries to solve a non-existent problem.

- The team members spend a great deal of time trying to complete this phase by themselves and lengthen the project completion time.

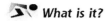 **What is it?** DMAIC

The purpose of the Define phase is to finalize the selection of a specific project, outline the objective, and determine the scope of the assigned work. The project leader and team members are assigned to the project. Together they assist the champion in defining the problem statement, project boundaries, and project milestones, and establish the criteria of success for the project, then document everything in a charter. The project champion, with help from the assigned project leader, should take the lead in this 6σ phase. (Note that the project leader may be a Master Black Belt, a Black Belt, or a Green Belt.)

To successfully launch the project team, the champion and the assigned project leader should strive to complete as much of the Define phase as possible before the team gets too far into the details of the project.

There are a far greater number of tools that could be employed in a project in the Define phase than those presented in this book. For example, some additional tools could be:

- **Project plan:** Provides a finer level of detail than just top-level milestones
- **Stakeholder analysis:** Helps the team understand the issues stakeholders may have related to the project

© 2015 GOAL/QPC

- **Financial analysis:** Helps justify the business case for the project
- **CTQ tree:** "Cascades" customer needs down to specific key process indicators (KPIs)

Step 1: Identify Voice of the Customer (VOC)

 ### What is it?

VOC analysis is the act of analyzing customer needs, wants, and expectations to help shape the scope and focus of the project. VOC data is collected and analyzed to determine what is driving customer satisfaction or dissatisfaction. Customers can be external, such as end users or purchasers of the product or service. Customers can also be internal to the process. Essentially whoever receives the output of your work is a customer. An important point to consider is that there is not just one VOC.

Why do it?

It is easy to assume you know what is important to your customers. However, projects often end up falling short on customer expectations because the customers' needs, wants, and expectations are not truly understood or they are misunderstood. It is important to understand not only what needs to be done better, but what is currently being done well. Work teams need to ensure that the company's processes continue to work well, and they also need to look for ways to correct deficiencies in their processes.

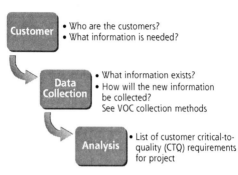

Customer
• Who are the customers?
• What information is needed?

Data Collection
• What information exists?
• How will the new information be collected? See VOC collection methods

Analysis
• List of customer critical-to-quality (CTQ) requirements for project

Tip: Consider customer segmentation by: revenue, geographic region, product usage, internal versus external customers, etc.

VOC Collection Methods

Interviews	Focus Groups	Surveys	Complaint Databases	Point of Use Observation	Competitors	Industry Literature	Customer Service Rep.

Tip: Organizations usually have access to a lot of customer information internally. Remember to leverage this data before seeking new information.

Tip: Surveys are commonly used and can be implemented by mail, e-mail, telephone, or face to face. Consider cost, speed of collection, and response rates when you are making a determination of which method to use.

If you don't use a standardized script or format, data will be collected inconsistently.

Step 2: Conduct Project Selection

What is it?

Project selection deals with the steps and methods used to select the Six Sigma project that the Green/Black Belts and other team members will be assigned to.

Why do it?

Organizations have limited resources. They need to have their Six Sigma teams working on projects that are most important to the needs of the organization. To do this, organizations need to take a structured approach.

 ## *How do I do it?*

1. Start by understanding:

   - **Voice of the Business (VOB)**
     What does the business say it needs?

   - **Voice of the Customer (VOC)**
     What do customers say they need?

   - **Voice of the Process (VOP)**
     What does available data say about current performance?

2. Assess project ideas already captured.

3. Prioritize the project list. Some possible tools to use are:

   - Financial Return on Investment (ROI)

   - Cause & Effect Diagram (C&E)

   - Failure Mode and Effects Analysis (FMEA)

   - Quality Function Deployment (QFD)

   - PICK Chart

For example: One organization's steering council has identified four projects for possible assignment to a 6σ project leader (MBB, BB, or GB) and team. The champion used a PICK Chart to rank the four projects, and then to select the correct project to assign to a team.

PICK Chart

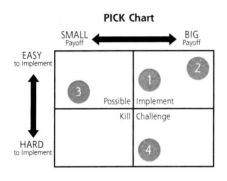

Projects 1 and 2 will be easy to implement and have a big payoff. They are viable projects to move forward with. Project 3 will be reasonably easy to implement, but will have a small payoff. It may be a possible option. While Project 4 will have a big payoff, it will be hard to implement. Success will be challenging.

Tip: If you need a more detailed way to discriminate between projects, you can use a 1–10 scale to rank "payoff" (rather than small versus big payoff), and the same 1–10 scale for "ease of implementation" (rather than easy versus hard to implement). 1 could equal small payoff or hard to implement, 5 could equal medium payoff or medium difficulty to implement, and 10 could equal big payoff or easy to implement.

Step 3: Create Project Charter

What is it?

A project charter is the agreement between the business champion and the team. It spells out the problem statement and the performance standards for the project. Performance standards are: goals, (expected results, customers' criteria for acceptance, and deliverables), timing (timelines with deadlines and milestones), scope (project priorities and ground rules of engagement), resources (spending and staffing considerations), risk tolerance, and communication requirements (required reviews, reports, and approvals). The project charter can be loosely considered as the project contract.

Why do it?

The charter transfers authority from the champion to the team to do the project. Having a written document adds credibility to the team and acts as a communication tool to keep the team aligned with the wishes of the champion. It also defines the boundaries of the project and scope, which help to keep the project on track by avoiding additional work being added to the project (called scope creep).

How do I do it?

1. Create a problem statement.

   - Common practice is to capture information regarding: When has the problem occurred? What is the defect? What is the magnitude of the defect? How much pain has the organization experienced because of the problem or defect? Pain is often expressed as "cost of poor quality."

2. Document project goals.

   - Goals are often stated as a significant reduction in defect rate, or waste (cost and time over what is needed). Challenge the team to consider a 50–70% reduction in the defect rate or in the amount of waste.

3. Describe the business case.
   - Often based on annual savings
4. Determine the resources needed.
5. Identify in-scope and out-scope elements and process boundaries.
6. Establish milestones, tollgate reviews, progress reviews.

Charters can be updated and revised as the project moves forward, but scope should not be arbitrarily extended without considering needed adjustments in resources or project duration.

Project Charter Example

Problem Statement: During the previous year, the finishing department had a 5% scrap rate. This cost the company $250,000 for the year. In addition, customers are increasingly dissatisfied as late deliveries are occurring more frequently.

Goal Statement: Reduce scrap by half (50%) by the end of the 4th quarter.

Business Case: Reducing scrap by 50% has the potential to save the company $125,000 per year, not accounting for expenses. The project is estimated to require $25,600 of an investment. (This amount represents four team members at four hours per week for four months at an average labor rate of $100/hour.) No capital purchases should be required.

Resources:
- Green Belt as project leader
- Two Yellow Belts for data collection and support
- Quality engineer for support

Scope:
In-scope includes Production and Inspection Departments

Continued on next page

Out of scope is new equipment purchases and supplier's process.

Milestones:

Define	Month 0
Measure	Month 1
Analyze	Month 2
Improve	Month 3
Control	Month 4

Step 4: Assign Team

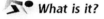 *What is it?*

The team is the group of people who will be supporting the person leading the project. Team membership may include subject matter experts on the process being improved or individuals who have a needed skill set, from areas like: accounting and finance, data collection, information technology, human resources, legal jurisdiction and law.

One way to structure team membership is to have some individuals on the core team, and other individuals on the extended team. Core team members would be those individuals who are needed to participate on the project from start to finish. Extended team members would agree to be available in providing support to the team as needed.

Why do it?

While the project leader may have some knowledge and expertise on the process being improved, the project leader's main task is to facilitate the team in using the 6σ tools. The scope of a project is often too large for just one person to be the team; and it has been proven time after time that a group of people arrive at a more creative and robust solution than just one person alone can.

How do I do it?

1. The champion and project leader determine what skill sets will be needed for the project.

2. The champion (and project leader, if needed) should solicit specific resources from the managers of the targeted areas.

3. Participation on the team should be incorporated into the organization's employee performance system.

Tip: For projects in manufacturing, a team size of 4–6 is common. For projects in the administrative areas of a business (or for a service-based organization), additional people may be needed if more functional areas of the business are included in the project scope.

Step 5: Create SIPOC

What is it?

SIPOC is a charting method for documenting the suppliers, the inputs, the process, the outputs, and the customers.

Why do it?

In Six Sigma, the team is trying to solve the $y = f(x)$ relationship, where y = the output(s) of the process, and x = the input(s) of the process.

Using SIPOC to study a process is the starting point for the team to understand this relationship. Teams look at the SIPOC components to aid in their understanding of a process and its boundaries. Using SIPOC, the team identifies the inputs (x) coming into the process, the outputs (y) of the process, and the suppliers and customers of the process.

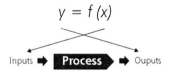

$$y = f(x)$$

Inputs ➡ **Process** ➡ Ouputs

A SIPOC acts as a communication device between the champion and the team to clarify to everyone the scope of work that could potentially be analyzed and considered for improvement.

The SIPOC serves as the starting point for creating a process map in the Measure phase.

🏃 How do I do it?

1. Identify the top-level process.

2. Determine the customers of the process.

3. Identify output(s) of the process (big Y's). There will also be outputs for each step in the process. These are referred to little y's. Your team will identify the little y's in the Measure phase when you create a process map.

4. Identify the inputs coming into the process (big X's). There will also be inputs for each step in the process. These are referred to little x's. Your team will identify the little x's in the Measure phase when you create a process map.

5. Determine the suppliers of the inputs.

6. To clarify scope and boundaries, identify the 4–8 steps that make up the process. These would be actual process steps and not decision blocks.

Tip: The SIPOC is the starting point for the team. A great deal of process knowledge is gained by having the whole team involved with the process-mapping activity.

Partial Charter Example

If a team received a charter based on reducing coffee brewing costs, a typical next step for the assigned project leader and team would be to develop a SIPOC for that process.

Problem Statement: During the year, costs for brewing coffee increased 100% over budget.

Goal Statement: Reduce coffee waste by half (50%) by the end of the month.

SIPOC Example

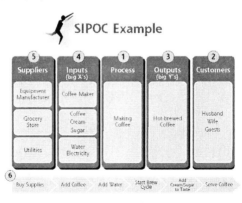

Chapter 2

DMAIC: Measure Phase

Typical Steps

Create Process Map
Conduct Measurement Systems Analysis
Collect Data
Calculate Basic Statistics
Calculate Six Sigma Capability Metrics

See the Advanced DMAIC section (Chapter 6, Green/Black-Belt-level tools) for information on measurement systems analysis (MSA).

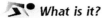

➤ What is it? DMAIC

The purpose of the Measure phase is to document the "as-is" or current process. The team, which was identified and assembled in the Define phase, will now be fully engaged in the project.

There are a far greater number of tools that could be employed in the Measure phase of a project than those presented in this book. For example, some additional tools could be:

- Cause and Effect Diagram: to funnel down to the more critical parts of the process.

- Pareto Analysis: to show which issues are occurring most frequently. (Chapter 3)

- Failure Mode and Effects Analysis (FMEA): to identify where the process is failing to meet expectations and the impact on the customer. (Chapter 4)

- Value Stream Map: to show the information, process, and material flows in a process. (Chapter 6)

- Control Chart: to calculate the statistical control limits of the outputs of a process. (Chapter 5)

Step 1: Create Process Map

What is it?

Creating a process map is typically the first activity in the Measure phase that the whole team works on. The steps of the process are documented, along with inputs and outputs for each step. It is a continuation of the SIPOC and may be done in multiple levels for efficiency.

The process map is a visual tool that allows a team to develop a clear understanding of the process. It is a key tool to help the team document the process baseline.

Why do it?

This activity helps to focus the team and generate needed information for other tools required in the project. For example:

- inputs and outputs are used in the FMEA
- data collection points are identified for the data collection plan
- points to where measurement system analysis may need to be used

How do I do it?

1. Start with the block diagram your team generated in the SIPOC. If your team doesn't have a diagram, create one, keeping to 4–8 steps of detail.

2. Add the output(s) to each step. (Little y's.)

3. Add the input(s) to each step. (Little x's.) Example: An input or big X of a process (SIPOC) might be a milling machine. A little x might be the spindle speed of the milling machine.

4. Classify the inputs as:

   - **Controllable (C)** Inputs in the process that can be set as specified.

   - **Noise (N)** Inputs that can't be controlled or are not feasible to control.

   - **Standard Operating Procedure (S)** Written and unwritten documentation specifying the application sequence for multiple inputs.

   - **Critical (CR)** According to the analysis conducted.

   Inputs are classified to document and share the understanding of what might be easy to change (controllable versus noise), what procedures are involved (SOP), and whether any of the inputs are determined to be critical (CR).

Tip: Approach the mapping activity in levels. Pick the critical steps in the first level and create a second-level map for those steps. As the team drills into the process and gets into the Analyze and Improve phases, it may be useful to develop a flowchart to understand decisions, value-added analysis, and handoffs in the work flow.

See *The Black Belt Memory Jogger*™ for additional details.

Process Map Example: Making Coffee

Outputs (little y's)

Correct Price Correct Quantity On Time	Correct Quantity	Correct Quantity	Correct Cycle Selected	Correct Quantity	On Time

Buy Supplies	Add Coffee	Add Water	Start Brew Cycle	Add Cream/Sugar to Taste	Serve Coffee
N Cream	C Coffee	N Water	S Directions	N Cream	N Operator
N Sugar	N Scoop	C Cup	N Operator	N Sugar	N Tray
C Coffee	C Cup	S Directions		N Cups	
N Buyer	S Directions	N Operator		N Operator	
	N Operator			S Coffee Drinker Input	

Inputs (little x's)

Continued on next page

If the "Buy Supplies" step was determined to be critical, a flowchart may be created to understand the details of the process step.

Coffee Example

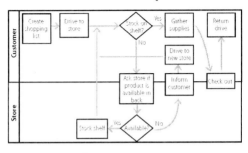

Step 2: Conduct Measurement Systems Analysis (MSA)

⟋⟍● *What is it?*

Measurement systems analysis is done with a collection of tools that validate the measurement process. Some of the tools are: calibration, gauge repeatability and reproducibility (GR&R), stability studies, and linearity studies. It is very common in the DMAIC process-improvement model that teams ensure the measurement system is repeatable and reproducible.

Repeatability is the amount of variation seen when one person takes multiple measurements using the same gauge on the same set of parts.

Reproducibility is the amount of variation seen when multiple people take measurements using the same gauge on the same set of parts.

Why do it?

Teams use data to make decisions. If the measurement system that is being used to collect the data is not accurate or not precise enough, then teams may make decisions based on incorrect data.

 ### How do I do it?

See the Green/Black-Belt-Level Tools (advanced DMAIC tools) in Chapter 6 Advanced Tools: Green/Black-Belt Level on how to conduct a measurement systems analysis.

Step 3: Collect Data

 ### What is it?

Most likely, your Six Sigma team will need to collect some data for your project. The team's plan for collecting data should outline the "what, where, and how" of the data collection activity.

Why do it?

It can be expensive for a team to collect more data than is needed, and a project could ultimately fail or have a diminished result if the proper data isn't collected. The Yellow Belt often plays a very critical role in collecting data for the project and needs to understand data collection techniques.

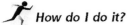

🏃 *How do I do it?*

1. Review the process map (or flowchart) for the data collection points.

2. Assess what data has already been collected.

3. Validate the measurement system (assess repeatability and reproducibility). Also see *The Black Belt Memory Jogger*™ for a detailed explanation of measurement systems analysis.

4. Create a data collection plan.

What to Measure?

A. What will you measure? Time? Distance? Number of defects? How many people were given service in a set amount of time? How many parts created by the hour?

B. Is what you will be measuring an output (Y) or input (X) measure? This information should be shown on the project team's process map. In the Analyze phase, to identify critical inputs, you will need to also capture all the relevant x's associated with the output.

C. An operational definition should describe the measure and how it is to be measured.

How to Measure It?

D. What is the measurement method?

- Is the method manual or automated?

- Does the measurement method require an instrument or gauge?
- Is there a test or standard operating procedure to reference?

E. How does the data collection need to be stratified? This information should come from the process map. Typically the data are some of the inputs or something about the input, e.g., the input may be "the operator," and something of interest about the operator is length of time on the job.

F. Who will collect the data?

G. Where will the data be collected?

H. When will the data be collected?

I. Determine the needed sample size. Discuss with a Green or Black Belt to determine the sample size needed for statistical validity.

Tip: Don't rule out manual data collection. Automation of data collection may not be needed or desired for the long term since it may only be needed during the project.

Elements of A Data Collection Plan

Define What to Measure			Define How to Measure					
Measure	Y/X	Operational Definition	Measurement Method	Stratification Factors	Who	Where	When	Sample Size
(A)	(B)	(C)	(D)	(E)	(F)	(G)	(H)	(I)

Tip: When you are designing forms for data collection, consider how the data will be collected and how it will be analyzed so that you can avoid wasting time during collection or in the manipulation of data after it is collected.

Example

What to measure?

Consider a project team at a Call Center that wants to monitor and reduce the number of calls the center receives.

- What is a call? Only those that connect? Those that drop because they have been on hold for too long?

- What about calls placed in error?

How does the data need to be grouped or stratified?

- How many calls are received in reference to a specific product or product line?

- What types of issues and defects are being reported?

- What day of the week are the calls? What time of day?

> **Tip:** Strive for consistency in the execution of the plan to ensure that data will be useful for analysis.

> **Tip:** If the measurement is not capable, then new and previously collected data may not be meaningful. Make sure the team verifies the measurement systems.

Step 4: Calculate Basic Statistics

 *What is it?*

Statistics are values that have been calculated from sample data. Statistics are estimates of the true population value (called parameters). Since the population is not typically understood, statistics are used. The Yellow Belt will encounter statistics for continuous and discrete data.

Data can be described as **_continuous_** if it can be broken down into measurements less than a whole unit. **Examples:** Length, weight, temperature. Continuous data is also referred to as variable data.

Data can be described as **_discrete_** if the data can't be broken down to less than a whole unit. **Examples:** Number of defects, number of calls received, number of complaints. Sometimes data of this type is referred as attribute data.

For continuous (variable) data, measurements are:

- Mean
- Median
- Mode
- Standard deviation
- Variance
- Range

For discrete (attribute) data, measurements are:

- Attribute (binary, e.g., good/bad, pass/fail, high/low, etc.)
- Nominal (categorical classification)
- Ordinal (ordered, e.g., 1st, 2nd, 3rd)
- Count (e.g., count of number of defects)

For examples of how to calculate statistics for discrete data, see the section called "Calculate Six Sigma Capability Metrics" in this chapter.

Why do it?

The purpose of calculating basic statistics is to characterize the "as-is" or current process. For example, your team will find out: What is the average output of the process? What is the standard deviation of the process? Your team can use the baseline information to understand the gap from desired performance and to gauge how much the process can be improved. Basic statistics are calculated not

---

only in the Measure phase, but as required throughout the DMAIC cycle. Basic statistics are, as are other tools, an important part of data analysis.

 ## How do I do it?

For continuous data, you need to calculate the location (center) and the variation in the data to fully understand it.

Measures of Location

Mean = the average of a set of data. Add up all the values in a set of data and divide by the number of data points.

Median = The midpoint of the data. If the data is sorted from low to high, it is the middle value when there is an odd number of points. When there is an even number, the two middle points are added and then divided by 2.

Mode = the most frequently occurring value.

Example

A project team at a Call Center has measured the time in minutes it takes to set up a customer account. The team wants to create the statistical baseline for the length of time of this set up.

Given the data of set-up time in minutes:

23, 22, 25, 19, 22, 24, 24, 20, 22, 18, 21

Mean $= \bar{x} = \frac{\Sigma x}{n} = \frac{(23+22+25+19+22+24+20+22+18+21)}{10} = 21.6$

Sorted data: 18 19 20 21 $\boxed{22 \ 22}$ 22 23 24 25

Median $= \frac{22 + 22}{2} = 22$

Mode $= 22$

> **Tip:** The sample size needs to be large enough to have statistical validity. A Green or Black Belt can help you determine the appropriate size. The small sample shown here is just for demonstration. A good rule of thumb is to collect at least 30 data points.

Measures of Variation

Standard deviation (s) = Measure which calculates the amount of variation around the mean.

$$S = \hat{\sigma} = \sqrt{\frac{\Sigma(x - \bar{x})^2}{n - 1}}$$

Variance = the standard deviation squared = $\hat{\sigma}^2$
Range = largest value − smallest value

In the formula, the deviation from the mean is squared and is divided by n −1 (n is the number of data points in the group). The square root is then taken, resulting in the sample standard deviation.

Example

The project team at the Call Center has measured the time (in minutes) it takes to set up a customer account. The team wants to create the statistical baseline for the variation in set-up time.

Data Point	X Value	X − Average	$(X - Average)^2$
1	23	1.4	1.96
2	22	0.4	0.16
3	25	3.4	11.56
4	19	-2.6	6.76
5	22	0.4	0.16
6	24	2.4	5.76
7	20	-1.6	2.56
8	22	0.4	0.16
9	18	-3.6	12.96
10	21	-0.6	0.36

Average = 21.6

Sum of each $(X - Average)^2$	42.4
Divided by n − 1	4.71
Take square root to get the standard deviation	2.17 minutes

Here is the same information shown in the formula for finding the average output of the process.

$$S = \hat{\sigma} = \sqrt{\frac{(23-21.6)^2 + (22-21.6)^2 + (25-21.6)^2 + \ldots (21-21.6)^2}{10-1}} = 2.17$$

Variance = $\hat{\sigma}^2 = 2.17^2 = 4.71$ minutes
Range = 25 − 18 = 7 minutes

Tip: In practice, the standard deviation is reported as the measure of variation since it represents the average amount of variation around the mean. In the example, the standard deviation is 2.17 minutes. The variance is 4.71 minutes^2. If you reported the variance to the boss, the boss would really be confused. The variance is in squared units.

Step 5: Calculate Six Sigma Capability Metrics

What is it?

The objective of the Measure phase is to characterize the process and create the baseline. Part of that baseline is understanding the process capability. The process capability metric provides a numerical quantification of the capability. The exact process capability metric to be used will depend on what kind of data you have and what metric the customer is asking for. There are metrics for continuous data, as well as discrete data.

Use Metrics that Match the Data

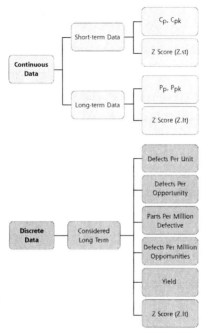

Note 1: The Z score is the sigma-level measure. The short-term Z score is used to report the sigma level. The long-term Z score can be converted to a short-term Z value. See *The Black Belt Memory Jogger*™ for a more complete description of this conversion and the C_p, C_{pk}, P_p, P_{pk} metrics.

Note 2: Some of the metrics shown in the diagram above are based on the concept of an opportunity. An opportunity is defined as a chance for a nonconformance. The total opportunities would be a count of all the ways for a defect to occur.

Why do it?

The purpose of using capability metrics in the Measure phase is to document the baseline of the as-is process. These baseline measures provide the basis to determine the level of improvement that might be required in the process, as well as the amount of improvement that could be realized at the end of the project.

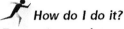 *How do I do it?*

For continuous data:

1. Determine if the measurement system is capable. Improve as required.

2. If the data is available, and collected via a capable measurement system, utilize historical data from the process to calculate process capability. If not, collect new data.

3. For continuous data, confirm the data is normally distributed. If not, stratification and non-normal capability techniques may be needed. Normality is not an assumption for discrete data.

4. Calculate the Z score using the formula below. A Z score of 3 or 4 is interpreted as average capability. A Z score of 6 is considered world-class capability.

$$Z \text{ Score} = \frac{X - \overline{X}}{S}$$

Example

The team at the Call Center wants to determine sigma level capability for setting up customer accounts. It was previously determined that the average time was 21.6 minutes and the standard deviation was 2.17 minutes. The upper specification limit (USL) =30 minutes.

$$Z \text{ Score} = \frac{30 - 21.6}{2.17} = 3.9$$

5. Assess capability. Many factors need to be considered when assessing whether the capability is adequate. For example:

- What is the current cost of poor quality (COPQ)?

- Is your organization or team meeting customer requirements?

- What would be the cost to improve the capability?

For discrete data:

Defects per Unit (DPU) = $\dfrac{\text{\# of defects}}{\text{Total \# of units}}$

Defects per Opportunity (DPO) = $\dfrac{\text{\# of defects}}{(\text{Total \# of units}) \times (\text{\# of opp's})}$

Parts per Million defective (PPM) = DPU × 1,000,000

Defects per Million Opportunities (DPMO) = DPO × 1,000,000

Yield = 1 − DPU (where there is one opportunity per unit, and an approximation where opportunities are > 1)

Example

The team at the Call Center wants to determine the defects per million opportunities or DPMO incurred while processing customer claims. The claim form contains 15 key pieces of information. The team counted 200 defects during the processing of 2,500 customer claims.

$$\text{DPMO} = \frac{200}{2{,}500 \times 15} \times 1{,}000{,}000 \cong 5{,}333$$

Tip: Defects per unit or DPU is often preferred over defects per opportunity or DPO, since specifying the number of opportunities can be at times subjective and easily manipulated. DPU is a measure that ties more closely with the customer experience. However, DPO/DPMO accounts for complexity and can be a good measure for management studies.

For both continuous and discrete data, the sigma level (Z score) can be computed. The Z score is the variable from the standard normal distribution. A standard normal distribution has a mean of 0 and a standard deviation of 1. It represents the number of standard deviations between the mean and a given value (usually a specification limit).

See Appendix A for the full conversion table for sigma level to yield (percentage free of defects).

Sigma Level to Yield Conversion

(extracted from Appendix A)

Sigma Level $_{ST}$	DPMO $_{LT}$	Yield $_{LT}$
4.2	3,467	99.6555%
4.1	4,661	99.5339%
4.0	6,210	99.3790%
3.9	8,108	99.190%

LT = Long Term
ST = Short Term

To understand the Call Center's DPMO of 5,333 for processing customer claims, in terms of a sigma level (in the short term), the team consulted the "Sigma Level to Yield Conversion" chart. For 5,333 DPMO, the sigma level is approximately 4.05. By convention the sigma level (in the short term) is the number reported.

Chapter 3

DMAIC: Analyze Phase

Typical Steps

| Identify Sources of Variation |
| Use Graphical Analysis for Screening |
| Use Statistical Analysis to Identify Critical Inputs (X's) |

If the Analyze phase is skipped or is done only superficially, significant issues can result later in the project, such as:

- The Improve phase may fail to yield a solution since it is not known what is critical.

- Excessive cost and/or time may occur in the Improve phase due to not analyzing available data.

Note: Some of the common statistical techniques and tools are briefly discussed in the Green/Black-Belt-Level Tools section in Chapter 6.

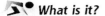

What is it?

The purpose of the Analyze phase is to identify the critical inputs to the process, which can be used to develop a solution in the Improve phase. This is accomplished by conducting a deeper dive into the process, and then using various graphical and statistical tools to verify key relationships and root causes of the problem.

While Green Belts do get statistical training, they often rely on Black Belts (or Master Black Belts) to help with the more complicated data analysis. This section discusses some of the simpler tools that a Yellow Belt might be called upon to do or be directly involved with. There are a far greater number of tools that could be employed in the Analyze phase of a project than those presented in this book. For example, some additional tools could be:

- Layout diagrams (also called Spaghetti Charts) to map people/material/information flow

- 2nd level process maps or flowcharts

- Failure Mode and Effects Analysis (FMEA)

- Advanced statistical tools like Analysis of Variance (ANOVA), Regression, Chi-square analysis, Logistic regression

---

- Statistical Process Control (SPC) on the little x's and little y's
- Measurement Systems Analysis (MSA) on the little x's

Step 1: Identify Sources of Variation

What is it?

In the Measure phase, teams identify process inputs as part of the mapping activity. These inputs, or some aspect of the inputs, may contribute to the variation in the output. The following tools help to supplement the team's mapping activity (done in the Measure phase) so the team can now identify additional inputs or dive deeper into the inputs already identified.

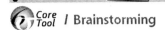

Core Tool / Brainstorming

What is it?

Brainstorming is a process to help generate ideas for a given topic. It could be used to generate a list of potential causes of a problem or potential solutions.

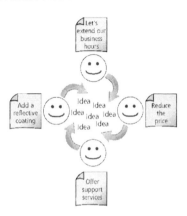

Why do it?

A higher volume of ideas can be generated by a team than can be done by a single individual.

Also, the quality of the ideas can be better as people can build off of the ideas generated by others.

🏃 How do I do it?

1. Identify the topic or problem.

2. Clarify the issue and provide any needed background information to the group.

3. Ideas can be delivered in turn by each member of the group (structured approach) or randomly by any member of the group (unstructured approach).

   Tip: Go for quantity over quality.

   Tip: Do NOT criticize any ideas.

   Tip: Feel free to build on others' ideas.

4. Continue with the process until the ideas per person are exhausted.

   Tip: If using a structured approach, use a time limit per team member to keep the process moving and to help generate ideas quickly.

5. Review the list for duplicates and remove them.

- After the session has concluded, if a large number of ideas have been generated, organize the ideas into similar categories. A common theme should emerge and the groups can be labeled accordingly. This is known as an Affinity Diagram.

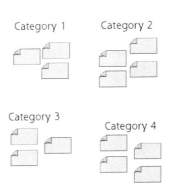

Category 1   Category 2

Category 3   Category 4

Core Tool / Non-Value-Added Analysis

What is it?

Non-value-added activities are those that:

- the customer doesn't want to pay for.
- don't transform the product or service.
- are not done right the first time.

These non-value-added activities can often be grouped into categories of the 8 Wastes.

The 8 Wastes

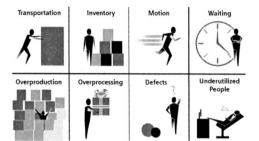

| Transportation | Inventory | Motion | Waiting |
| Overproduction | Overprocessing | Defects | Underutilized People |

Why do it?

Having non-value-added activities can result in extra cost and time for any organization. Removal of these activities helps to increase the *velocity* of the product or transaction or service and reduce the ultimate cost to the customer.

Velocity refers to how quickly the product moves through the process. The product doesn't stop the process to be added to inventory in the warehouse, it isn't needlessly transported around the factory, it isn't being reworked, and so on.

It is not uncommon for up to 95% of the cycle time of a process to be consumed by waste.

How do I do it?

1. Develop the flowchart of work steps from the process map developed during the Measure phase.

   • This is usually a 2nd or 3rd level of mapping detail.

2. Identify each step as value added (VA), business-value added (BVA), or non-value added (NVA). The BVA category is also sometimes called non-value added but necessary.

Examples of VA, NVA, and BVA

Service

Value added (VA)	Food preparation
Non-value added (NVA)	Transporting food
Business-value added (NVA but necessary)	Compliance with government regulations

Manufacturing

Value added (VA)	Drilling a hole
Non-value added (NVA)	Reworking a defect
Business-value added (NVA but necessary)	Performing inspection that is contractually required

3. Review each NVA step to determine if it can be removed or minimized.

Example of Process Map with Flowchart

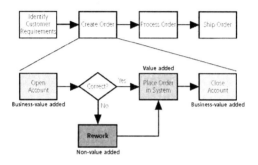

Tip: Adding a color scheme to the flowchart can provide a quick view to management on how much of the process is non-value added.

Step 2: Use Graphical Analysis for Screening

➤ What is it?

After the team identifies all the potential variables in the process, graphical analysis can be conducted to screen out the more critical inputs from the rest.

This funneling strategy helps teams to prioritize the inputs for additional analysis.

The exact graphical tool a team selects will depend on the stated problem or the question being asked and the type of data the team has. As will be seen, some graphs will require having continuous data while others will have discrete data.

Typical graphical tools used are:

- Box Plot
- Histogram
- Run Chart
- Scatter Diagram
- Cause & Effect Diagram
- Pareto Chart
- 5 Whys

Why do it?

Graphical tools are commonly used in the Analyze phase to screen variables for importance before statistical analysis is conducted.

Both graphical and statistical tools are usually done with software. However, if you or your team wants to construct the tools manually, *The Black Belt Memory Jogger* ™ is a good resource for learning additional tools and details.

 *Core Tool* / Box Plot

 What is it?

Box Plots summarize a set of numerical data. They are most useful in comparing several data sets for central tendency and variation.

Box Plot Data from Call Center

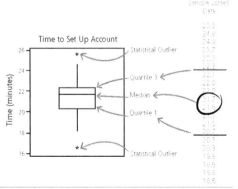

How do I do it?

1. Collect numerical data and arrange in a single column (or multiple columns if several Box Plots are to be created for comparison).

2. Sort data from high to low and divide it into quartiles.

3. Draw whiskers out to the last data point or to 1.5 x (Q3 – Q1). Points beyond this are labeled as outliers. Q3 – Q1 is called the "inter-quartile range" (IQR).

IQR = Q3 – Q1

Upper whisker threshold = Q3 + 1.5 (IQR)
Lower whisker threshold = Q1 – 1.5 (IQR)

Points above and below these thresholds are flagged as outliers.

 Core Tool / Histogram

What is it?

Histograms are used to view the shape and spread of a set of data. Data sets >50 are generally needed to develop a reasonable understanding of the distribution.

Histogram of Time vs. Frequency

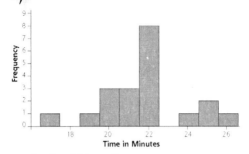

Data from Call Center. Time to set up customer account.

How do I do it?

1. Collect a numerical sample of data and arrange in a single column of numerical data (or multiple columns if several Histograms are to be created for comparison).

2. Determine the range of the data set.

3. Determine bin size. One method to start with is to set the number of bins to: # of bins = $\sqrt{n}$ rounded to the next whole value, where n = the sample size.

4. Plot the data per the bin ranges calculated. Count the number of data points in each bin and make the bar the height of the count.

5. Analyze the shape and spread of the data.

> **Tip:** Bin sizes can be modified. Smaller data sets may be more understandable with fewer bins, and larger data sets may require more. Statistical software will calculate an appropriate bin size automatically.

It is generally advantageous for the team to understand the shape of the data when it is plotted. Many statistical tools are available for normally distributed data, and often non-normally-distributed data will provide clues on how the process is operating.

Standard Normal Distribution

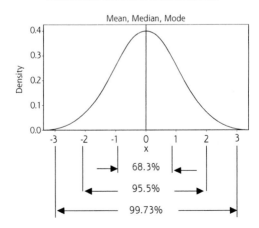

Data that are normally distributed will plot symmetrically around the mean. In addition, the mean, median, and mode will be the same value. Plotting a Histogram will give you a sense of the shape of the data. Items to look for:

Skewness:

Tail drags to right—
Positive skewed

Tail drags to the left—
Negative skewed

Data may naturally be skewed, or have over-lapping populations.

Kurtosis:

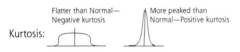

Flatter than Normal—
Negative kurtosis

More peaked than
Normal—Positive kurtosis

Data may naturally exhibit these characteristics, or have overlapping populations.

Multi-Modal:

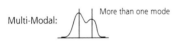

More than one mode

Look for overlapping populations.

> **Tip:** Normal distributions are usually characterized by the mean and standard deviation. Taking +/- 3 standard deviations around the mean represents the amount of variation that would be expected over time.

Core Tool / Run Chart

What is it?

Run Charts are used to study data collected over time. Generally >20 data points are needed to understand patterns in the data.

Standard Run Chart

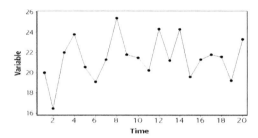

How do I do it?

1. Collect data for the numeric characteristic of interest.

2. Plot the data, preserving the time sequence.

3. Analyze the chart for patterns.

Patterns to look out for:

Run Chart: Shifts

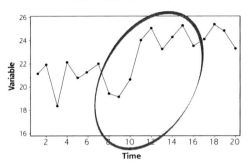

Run Chart: Trends

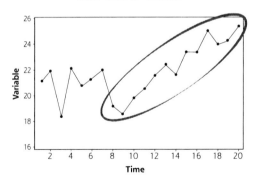

Run Chart: Unusual Data Points

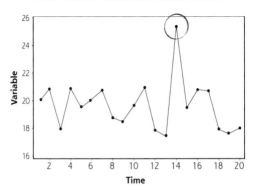

Run Chart: Increases and Decreases in Variation

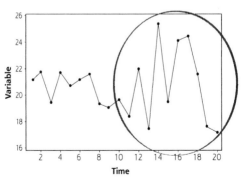

> **Tip:** Adding the centerline to the data can
> help you to see patterns. A Control Chart
> (in place of a Run Chart) can also help you
> to see patterns in the data as well, and
> provide some additional diagnostics.

Core Tool / Scatter Diagram

What is it?

Scatter Diagrams identify possible relationships
between numeric variables. Potential
relationships could be linear or curvilinear.

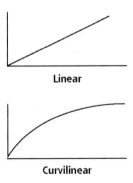

Linear

Curvilinear

Scatter Diagrams are often done in advance of
correlation and regression analysis (instructions
for which are beyond the scope of this book.)

Scatter Diagram

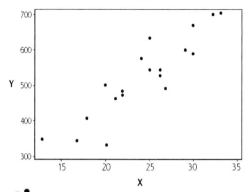

How do I do it?

1. Collect paired numeric data. Use >50 paired samples of data.

Some Data Points for Coffee Example

Row	# of Cups of Coffee	Minutes to Consume
1	1	15
2	1.5	20
3	1.25	19
4	1.5	25
5	2	32
6	2	35
7	3	42

2. Plot the data on a graph. Traditionally, the independent variable (input or predictor) is placed on the X axis, and the dependent variable (output or predicted) on the Y axis. However, a visual relationship between the variables does not imply one causes the other. A third variable might be responsible for the change in Y value, and/or the X value.

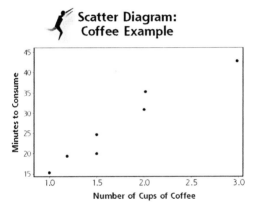

Scatter Diagram: Coffee Example

3. Analyze the graph.

Scatter Diagram: No Correlation

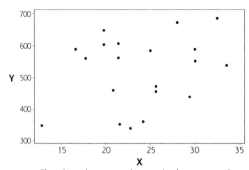

There is no demonstrated connection between x and y.

Scatter Diagram: Positive Correlation

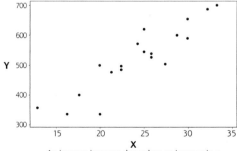

An increase in y may depend on an increase in x.

Scatter Diagram: Negative Correlation

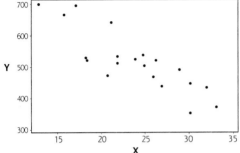

X

A decrease in y may depend on an increase in x.

4. To quantify the strength of the relationship, the correlation coefficient "r" or the coefficient of determination "R^2" can be calculated. Consult a Green or Black Belt to understand how to calculate the coefficient "r" or "R^2."

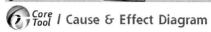

⑦ Core Tool / Cause & Effect Diagram

What is it?

Cause and Effect Diagrams help teams identify, capture, and organize potential causes related to a problem.

Also known as:

- Ishikawa Diagram
- Fishbone Diagram

Cause & Effect Diagram Example of Call Center Issues

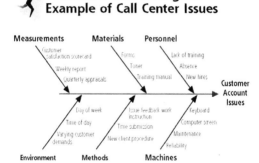

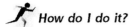

How do I do it?

1. Determine the categories to use for the major cause categories. Typically, a format similar to the example is used (Measurements, Materials, Man or Personnel, Mother Nature or Environment, Methods, and Machines) or the "process classification" method of using the major process steps is used.

2. Define the effect or problem and record it on the diagram as the head of the "fish."

3. Capture the potential causes with brainstorming or from actual process data by recording the ideas/pieces of data on the "bones" or skeleton of the fish.

4. Assign the potential causes to a category. (The categories are typically the six M's as mentioned in Step 1 or the major process steps your team has identified.)

Tip: The names of the categories can be modified to best represent the process under consideration and the culture of the organization. You can combine 5 Why analysis with C&E Diagrams to drill deeper into the causes.

Tip: The C&E Diagram could be used in the Define phase to provide focus for the project.

Core Tool / Pareto Chart

🎯 What is it?

A Pareto Chart is a bar chart that is sorted in descending order, from the tallest bar on the left of the chart, to the smallest bar on the right of the chart. The chart shows the frequency of a problem and the percentage of that problem out of 100%. The Pareto Chart can be used in the Define phase to determine what process to focus the project on, or in the Measure and Analyze phases to focus on the main cause of the problem.

How do I do it?

1. Determine the problem to focus on.

2. Use existing data, or brainstorm which causes will be monitored.

3. Determine if frequency or cost would be the best unit of measurement. Or do both.

4. Determine the time period for the study.

5. Gather the data.

6. Determine the frequencies and percentages.

7. List the causes in descending order, with the most frequent problem on the left, and the least frequent problem on the right.

9. Plot frequencies and percentages.

Pareto Chart Example

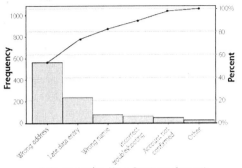

Process: Setting Up a Customer Account

	Wrong address	Late data entry	Wrong name	Incorrect troubleshooting	Account not confirmed	Other
Freq.	534	230	95	80	66	27
%	51.7	22.3	9.2	7.8	6.4	2.6
Cum %	51.7	74.0	83.2	91.0	97.4	100.0

> **Tip:** Commonly 20% of the causes will account for 80% of the problems. Use the Pareto Chart to separate the "vital few" issues from the "trivial many."

Tip: A multi-level Pareto Chart can be developed by creating a Pareto Chart for the drivers of the first, tallest bar in the Pareto Chart. This can be repeated for each successive bar until root causes are reached.

Example: the graphic "Pareto Chart of Wrong Address" shows a breakdown of the tallest bar (wrong address) in the main Pareto Chart.

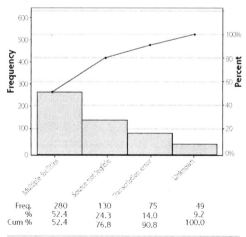

Pareto Chart of Wrong Address

	Multiple facilities	Source not legible	Transcription error	Unknown
Freq.	280	130	75	49
%	52.4	24.3	14.0	9.2
Cum %	52.4	76.8	90.8	100.0

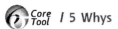

Core Tool / 5 Whys

What is it?

It is a simple technique that can be used to help a team arrive at a root cause by diving deeper into the cause and effect relationship related to the problem.

How do I do it?

1. Start with the potential causes identified in the Cause & Effect Diagram.

2. Ask "Why does this happen?"

3. Continue this "Why does this happen" questioning until a root cause is reached. It is not required that your team use all 5 Whys, but alternatively, your team may need to inquire deeper than five levels to get to the root cause of a problem.

> **Tip:** Use data to support the rationale for drilling down to the next level of cause. A common failure mode is that teams fail to use data to validate the cause and effect relationship.

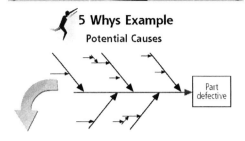

5 Whys Example
Potential Causes

Part defective

1. Why did the supplier ship a defective part?
   The required specification wasn't on the customer's printout.

2. Why wasn't the required specification on the customer printout?
   Engineer didn't specify requirement.

3. Why didn't the engineer specify the requirement?
   Engineer didn't know it had to be specified.

4. Why didn't engineer know to specify the requirement?
   Engineering manual not up to date.

5. Why isn't engineering manual up to date?
   Budget was cut last year and manual wasn't updated.

Step 3: Use Statistical Analysis to Identify Critical Inputs (X's)

What is it?

Statistical analysis encompasses various statistical tests that help teams validate relationships between the input(s) and the output of the process, or outputs of a step in the process. Very often it is done with samples of data, which is an inferential type of study.

Your team would use inferential statistics when you are trying to determine if the populations where the samples come from are significantly different from each other.

Why do it?

While graphs help Green and Black Belts to see relationships between the inputs and outputs, graphs cannot show whether the relationships are statistically significant or if there's random noise in the data, so therefore teams use statistical analysis to identify the critical inputs of a process.

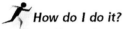 **How do I do it?**

For the Yellow Belt, it will be best to consult with the Green or Black Belt leading the project as to the type of analysis that should be conducted. However, some general steps follow.

1. From the graphical analysis, determine which input/output relationships to analyze. Start with relationships where the input appears to have a large impact on the output.

2. Determine if the input and output data is continuous or discrete.

Some examples:

Input	Output
Scenario 1	
Time (continuous)	Amount of chemical used (continuous)
Scenario 2	
Cleaned: Yes/No (discrete)	Test passed: Yes/No (discrete)
Scenario 3	
Machine A/B (discrete)	Surface finish (continuous)
Scenario 4	
Overtime hours (continuous)	Order shipped on time: Yes/No (discrete)

3. Select the appropriate test (see Hypothesis Testing, Chapter 6) based on the analysis objective and the type of data that is available.

4. Conduct the analysis and create the statistical model.

5. Reduce the model by removing inputs that are not statistically significant.

6. Analyze the residuals. Residuals are the deviations from the individual data points to the expected value determined by the model.

Chapter 4

DMAIC: Improve Phase

Typical Steps

| Develop Solution |
| Mistake Proof Solutions |
| Pilot Solution |

If the Improve phase is skipped or is done only superficially, significant issues can result later in the project, such as:

• An optimal solution may not get developed.

• The solution may not be validated before being released to the customer.

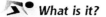

What is it?

The Analyze phase determined which variables are critical to address. The purpose of the Improve phase is to develop the best solution to the problem and to confirm the solution will work as intended. This phase uses a mix of quality and statistical tools to arrive at an appropriate solution.

There are a far greater number of tools that could be employed in the Improve phase of a project than those presented in this book. For example some additional tools could be:

- Designed experiments
- Simulation
- Regression modeling
- Kaizen events

Step 1: Develop Solution

Some commonly used tools for developing a solution in the Improve phase are: FMEA (Failure Mode and Effects Analysis), setup reduction, continuous flow, and a Solution Selection Matrix. These tools help Green and Black Belts to do a deeper dive into the issues causing the problem, provide a tracking mechanism for closing out issues, reducing the time it takes to switch between different products or services, and a way to evaluate competing solutions.

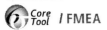

Core Tool / FMEA

What is it?

Failure Mode and Effects Analysis (FMEA) is a tool to help identify the most likely failure modes and their effects on the customer. It also identifies the frequency of occurrence and what controls are in place to prevent the cause(s) of the problem from happening again. The FMEA can be started in the Measure or Analyze phase for the "as-is" or current-state process. The team uses the FMEA to drill deeper into the process during the Analyze phase. During the Improve phase, the team uses FMEA to evaluate the "to-be" or future-state process.

Why do it?

The FMEA tool helps a team to track the critical issues during the project and it helps to prioritize the team's efforts. FMEA is a core Six Sigma tool that will directly involve the Yellow Belt.

How do I do it?

1. List the steps of the process from the process map. Start with the most critical steps first. This can be based on data or team knowledge.

2. List the failure modes that could occur. Failure modes are all the ways in which the output (Y) could fail to be achieved. The outputs are seen on the process map.

Tip: Each process step could have multiple failure modes.

3. List the effect of the failure mode on the customer. The customer could be internal or external to the organization.

   Tip: Each failure mode could have multiple effects.

4. List the potential causes. Causes are usually closely related to the process inputs. Inputs can be viewed on the process map.

   Tip: Each failure mode could have multiple causes.

5. Identify the current controls in the process. Controls would either prevent or detect the cause of the failure.

   Tip: Each cause could have multiple control and detection mechanisms.

   Tip: Each combination of failure mode, cause, and control would have a unique line in the FMEA.

Tip: Do steps 2 through 5 for a given process step and then repeat for the next process step.

6. On a scale from 1–10, where 1 is low and 10 is high, determine the severity of the failure effect on the customer.

Tip: For more detail on the 1–10 scale, see the table below.

Example of a Scoring Scale

Score	Severity Criteria	Occurrence		Detection
10	Hazardous without warning	1 in 2	Very high	Absolute uncertainty
9	Hazardous with warning	1 in 3	Very high	Very remote
8	Very high	1 in 8	High	Remote
7	High	1 in 20	High	Very low
6	Moderate	1 in 80	Moderate	Low
5	Low	1 in 400	Moderate	Moderate
4	Very low	1 in 2,000	Moderate	Moderately high
3	Minor	1 in 15,000	Low	High
2	Very minor	1 in 150,000	Low	Very high
1	None	1 in 1,500,000	Remote	Almost certain

For more information on constructing this chart, refer to *The Six Sigma Memory Jogger*™ *II*.

7. On a scale from 1–10, where 1 is rarely and 10 is often, determine the probability of occurrence of the cause.

---

8. On a scale from 1–10, where 1 is effective and 10 is ineffective, determine how effective the current controls are in detecting or preventing the cause of failure.

Tip: Columns to the left of the RPN column relate to the "as-is" process.

Tip: If permissible by your industry, it is helpful to create a customized 1–10 rating scale for severity, occurrence, and detection.

9. Calculate the risk priority number (RPN). The RPN = Severity x Occurrence x Detectability. With the traditional 1–10 scale, the resulting RPN will be a number from 1 to 1000.

Tip: Wait until steps 1 through 9 have been completed for most of the process before assigning recommended actions (step 10).

Tip: Sort the RPN column in descending order; this will facilitate focusing recommended actions on the most critical items.

10. Assign recommended actions to the highest RPNs. Start with the top 20% of the RPNs and continue to work down the list until the problems have been resolved.

11. Assign the actions to specific members of the team for resolution.

12. Determine due dates for the actions.

13. Record what action was taken to address the issue.

14. Record when the action was taken.

15. Calculate new predicted severities (PS), predicted occurrences (PO), and predicted detection (PD).

16. Calculate the new predicted RPN (PRPN).

Blank FMEA Chart

Steps 1	2	3	4	5	6	7	8	9	10	11	12	13	14	15	16
Part/Process	Failure Mode	Failure Effects	S	O	Causes	Controls	D	R P N	Action Recommended	Person Responsible	Schedule Date	Action Taken	Actual Completion Date	P P P S O D	P R P N

For more information on constructing this chart, refer to *The Six Sigma Memory Jogger™ II*.

FMEA Chart for Coffee Example

Steps 1	2	3	4	5	6	7	8	9	10	11	12	13	14	15	16
Part/Process	Failure Mode	Failure Effects	S	O	Causes	Controls	D	R P N	Action Recommended	Person Responsible	Schedule Date	Action Taken	Actual Completion Date	P P P S O D	P R P N
Buy supplies	Wrong coffee purchased	Return trip to store to return and re-buy	6	2	Shopping list incorrect	Standard checklist	2	24	None required					6 2 2	24
Buy supplies	Wrong coffee purchased	Return trip to store to return and re-buy	6	2	Wrong item selected from shelf	None	10	160	Add photo of product to checklist	Lead person	Nov 1st	Added photo	Oct 15th	6 3 1	18
Add coffee	Too much coffee	Strong coffee, customer will add cream or dilute	4	5	Variation in definition of "scoop"	Procedure	3	22	Modify procedure to define "scoop"	Supervisor	Oct 15th	Added definition and visual work instructions	Oct 15th	4 2 5	40
Add coffee	Too little coffee	Customer complains and asks for fresh coffee	8	5	Variation in definition of "scoop"	Procedure	3	163	Modify procedure to define "scoop"	Supervisor	Oct 15th	Added definition and visual work instructions	Oct 15th	8 2 5	80

RPN = Risk Priority Number
PS = Predicted Severity

PO = Predicted Occurrence
PD = Predicted Detection

PRPN = Predicted Risk Priority Number

Core Tool / Setup Reduction

⚡ What is it?

Setup (changeover) reduction is a technique teams use to evaluate all the elements of work performed during the set up of an activity, so they can develop ways to eliminate waste and reduce the overall time for the set-up activity. Set-up time is defined as the time from the last unit processed to the first good unit of the next product (service or transaction) produced on the same equipment.

Why do it?

By reducing set-up time, smaller batch sizes can be produced, making the organization more flexible and cost effective as work in process (WIP) is reduced.

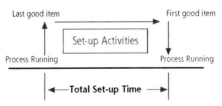

🏃 How do I do it?

1. Determine where to start setup reduction efforts.

   • First, look at bottleneck operations

- Second, work on process steps with the longest set-up times

2. Document the set-up activities.
   - Use flowcharts
   - Use video recordings of the set-up activities

3. Eliminate activities that do not need to be done.
   - Consider removing the non-value-added (NVA) steps and activities

4. Simplify the activities by making each step as simple as possible, using mistake proofing and standardization techniques.

5. Automate anything possible in the remaining tasks.

> **Tip:** Convert activities that are internal to the set up (when the process is stopped) to external (when the process is running) to reduce the time for set up and changeover.

Internal: Set-up activities are operations that can only be performed while the process or machine is stopped, e.g., die and tool exchange, tightening and loosening fasteners.

External: Set-up activities are operations that can be performed while the process or machine is running, e.g., locating hand tools, filling out paperwork, coordinating resources.

The concept of setup reduction can be easily understood by thinking about how a race car pit crew operates. As the car enters the pit, all the crew members are ready to spring into action. Each person has a specific task to do and he or she has all the needed materials available and ready to go. All unnecessary motion is eliminated and special tools are employed to reduce cycle time to the bare minimum.

Photo credit: Robert Doyle

Core Tool / Continuous Flow

What is it?

Continuous flow is where products are kept moving uninterrupted through the process. The ideal state of continuous flow is one-piece flow where items move one unit at a time, at a rate determined by customer requirements. It is often achieved by implementing a cellular design.

Why do it?

Moving from batch production to one-piece flow allows for more consistent delivery of product to the customer while minimizing work in process (WIP).

Given Process:

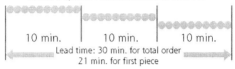

Batch & Queue Process with Batch Size = 10

| 10 min. | 10 min. | 10 min. |

Lead time: 30 min. for total order
21 min. for first piece

Same Process Using Continuous Flow

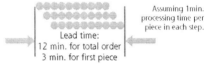

Assuming 1min. processing time per piece in each step.

Lead time:
12 min. for total order
3 min. for first piece

 How do I do it?

1. Determine the current process and customer requirements. Customer demand (often calculated as average daily demand), current process flow, process step cycle times, and *takt* time are often captured to better understand the current process and customer requirements.

   • *Takt* time, a German term made popular by the Japanese, is the time allowable to produce a part from start to finish in order to meet customer demand.

Example:

Takt time = available time divided by customer demand. Assume that customer demand is 100 units/day, and in an 8-hour shift there are 60 minutes of lunch and break time (during which time line workers are unavailable for production).

$$\text{Takt time} = \frac{7 \text{ hrs.} \times 60 \frac{\text{min.}}{\text{hr.}} \times 60 \frac{\text{sec.}}{\text{min.}}}{100 \text{ units}} = 252 \text{ sec./unit}$$

This means a unit should be produced on average every 252 seconds to meet customer demand.

2. Consider improved layout options. Should the flow be a straight line or in a U-shape configuration?

3. Identify and implement needed improvements with tools like non-value-added analysis, setup reduction, 5S, and visual management. (5S and visual management are described in Chapter 5.)

> **Tip:** One-piece flow is the ideal state and will not be possible in many situations.

> **Tip:** If designing a cell, counter-clockwise flow is often found to work efficiently for right-handed individuals.

Core Tool / Solution Selection Matrix

What is it?

In the Improve phase, solutions need to be identified and then prioritized for implementation. Some solutions will be obvious from the gaps in the current state maps (process maps, value stream maps, or flowcharts) or from the FMEA chart and can be quickly targeted for improvement. One common approach teams use to evaluate and prioritize solutions is to use a Solution Selection Matrix.

Why do it?

The Solution Selection Matrix helps teams identify the optimal solution(s) to implement, and not the first solutions that come to mind.

 How do I do it?

1. Identify the list of potential solutions. This list may come from team brainstorming, the process map, the FMEA chart, or a designed experiment.

2. Determine the criteria the team will use to evaluate the solutions. Some common criteria are:

   • Cost of implementation

   • Ease of implementation

   • Effectiveness of the solution

---

3. Use a scale from 1 to 10 to weight the criteria, based on how important the criteria are to the customer. A 10 can equal "most important" and a 1 "least important."

4. Assign a rank between 1 and 10 for each potential solution against each of the criteria.

5. Multiply the rating of importance (between 1 and 10) by the team's assigned score for the solution, and then sum the values.

   • Sort the final scores in descending order. Consider implementing the solutions with the highest scores.

Solution Selection Matrix Example

Rating of Importance to Customer		10	8	6	
		1	2	3	
Process Steps / Input Variables		Effectiveness	Cost	Ease	Total
1	Solution idea #1	5	6	8	146
2	Solution idea #2	10	8	8	212
3	Solution idea #3	3	5	7	112

10 = High Importance   1 = Low Importance

In this example, Solution #2 has the highest score of 212 and should be considered for implementation based on the criteria shown.

> **Tip:** Create definitions for the customer importance ratings.

Customer Importance Rankings and Corresponding Definitions

Ranking	Ease of Implementation	Cost of Implementation	Effectiveness of Solution
10	Easy	Low cost	High
5	Moderate	Moderate cost	Moderate
1	Hard	High cost	Low

Step 2: Mistake Proof Solution

 **Core Tool / Mistake Proofing**

➤ What is it?

Mistake proofing (also known as error proofing or poka-yoke) is a technique to help teams achieve zero defects by eliminating the errors or conditions that bring about the errors. If errors are prevented, then defects can't happen.

Why do it?

It will be more economical to prevent defects from being made than to produce products with defects, inspect products for defects, and then rework or produce new products to account for the defective items.

 How do I do it?

1. Identify the defect.

2. Map out the process steps that produce the defect.

3. Identify the errors that bring about the defect. Use 5 Whys, Pareto Charts, C&E Diagrams, FMEA, or more advanced root cause analysis tools (such as Fault Tree Analysis) to identify the error conditions.

4. Identify the purpose of mistake proofing: to provide warning, to stop the process from moving forward, or to control the process flow.

5. Determine the device or concept to be employed.

6. Pilot the mistake proofing to verify its effectiveness.

7. Adjust the mistake-proofing mechanism as needed.

Some mistake-proofing ideas:

- Color coding
- Varying the shape of parts or adding notches
- Checklists
- Templates
- Auto-detection (spell checking, formatted fields on computer forms)
- Contact sensors
- Motion sensors
- Counters
- Bar codes

Tip: It may also be helpful to consider how the mistake-proofing device will work. Elimination is best, but not always possible. Consider the other approaches in descending order.

Best Elimination: Eliminate the possibility of error.

Replacement: Use a more reliable process/technology.

Better Facilitation: Make the work easier to perform.

Detection: Detect the error before further processing.

Good Mitigation: Minimize the impact of the error.

Step 3: Pilot Solution

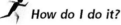 **What is it?**

A pilot is where the solution (or part of the solution) is introduced in a reduced implementation. Implementation could be limited to one plant, or one product. It could be limited by volume or time frame.

Why do it?

Pilots are done because the:

- scope of the change or solution may be too large to implement all at once.

- risk needs to be minimized.

- solution needs to be verified.

How do I do it?

1. Create a pilot plan. This includes who, what, when, where, and how.

2. Define the success criteria. Consider measures for both effectiveness of the solution and the efficiency of implementation (including training and communication).

3. Define the solution to be tested.

4. Execute the pilot plan.

5. Determine a process for capturing lessons learned by the team.

Tip: Communicate the pilot plan to all stakeholders.

Tip: Manage the pilot by taking an active role in understanding the details of the pilot plan and knowing how it is to be executed.

 Be aware that this is a pilot and not all may go per plan. Be ready to adapt.

Chapter 5

DMAIC: Control Phase

Typical Steps

Validate Improved Process Capability and Measurement System

Implement Process Controls

Complete Project Documentation

If the Control phase is skipped or is done only superficially, significant issues can result later, such as:

• Improved performance is not sustained.

• Financial results are not achieved.

• The process could actually be worse if budgets have been changed to reduce available resources and problems reemerge in the process.

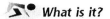

⚓ What is it?

The purpose of the Control phase is to put controls in place to sustain the project improvements (often in terms of improved process capability). Controls are documented in the control plan. A project team who has documentation for the new process can better ensure the transition of the new, improved process to the process owners.

Since process variation may have been significantly reduced during the project, the team should ensure the measurement system is still adequate for the application. The team, in addition to re-checking the measurement system, validates the project's financial benefit. Often this is done with the financial department.

Plans are developed, such as:

- Control plan
- Audit plan
- Training plan
- Documentation plan

Other project documentation might take the form of:

- Standard operating procedures
- Work instructions
- Lessons learned
- Final report

Step 1: Validate Improved Process Capability and Measurement System

As a project is nearing completion, the team needs to validate that the project has achieved the goal stated in the project charter. Most likely that goal was originally stated as an increase in process capability, or if it was stated as a cost reduction goal, the team likely targeted increasing process capability as a means to achieve the savings.

If you would like to review process capability, see Chapter 2. Also see Chapter 6, which describes some advanced process capability tools that Green and Black Belts use, but Yellow Belts should be familiar with.

Reevaluating the measurement system is also important to do at the end of the project. The team should have studied the measurement system during the Measure phase. If the measurement system was found to be deficient, then the team would have needed to make improvements to ensure it was adequate for the application. However, the measurement system may not be adequate at the end of the project due to all the improvements that were made to reduce variation.

Measurement Systems Analysis was discussed in Chapter 2 and is discussed further in Chapter 6.

Step 2: Implement Process Controls

 Core Tool / 5S

🎯 *What is it?*

5S is a methodology used to promote workplace housekeeping. 5S provides organization and stability for further process improvements. It can be a powerful tool to help sustain improvements. The 5S terms can be translated from the original Japanese words as: sort, store, shine, standardize, and sustain.

Why do it?

5S is done to put in place a clean, safe, organized, and productive workplace. It is a vital step in achieving a visually-managed workplace.

> **Tip:** Often the initial team effort goes into the first three S's, sort, store, and shine. The work on standardize and sustain typically happens over time.

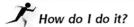

How do I do it?

1. **Sort:** Remove unneeded items from the workplace. Often a "red tag" process will be used to identify items to be removed after a designated time frame. Ultimately, unwanted items should be reassigned to another part of the business, sold, or thrown away. Also, work methods that are ineffective and should be "thrown away" can be replaced with best practices.

2. **Store:** Organize the remaining needed materials to minimize motion/transportation and other non-value-added waste. Everything should have a place or order (as in order of processing steps), and everything should be in its place or order.

3. **Shine:** Clean the current area to remove trash and possible contamination. Doing so will allow the team to see oil leaks, vibrations, and other unusual conditions in machines. Also, it will allow the team to see defects and other non-conformities in the process so that root causes of these conditions can be eliminated.

4. **Standardize:** Develop the procedures for how sort, store, and shine are to be done. A standardized process will clearly show the workforce where items go, and how to keep the work area free from unnecessary material and other distractions.

5. Sustain: The 5S culture needs to be sustained over time. Typically, management will arrange for audits to be conducted to evaluate how well the organization is conforming to the 5 S's. The results of the audit are documented and tracked.

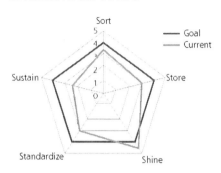

Core Tool / Visual Management

What is it?

Visual management is a set of visual techniques that help teams to see the status of production, visual controls, standards, and performance indicators.

Why do it?

Visual management is a way to standardize and share production information and performance feedback, often preventing the

need for meetings. This visual system of communication allows for anyone to develop a quick understanding of the current status of the process and parts of the process.

🏃 How do I do it?

1. Provide stability in the system by introducing 5S.

2. Identify current:
   - Standards
   - Work instructions
   - Production schedule
   - Process controls

3. Determine needed visual management controls to install. Some examples are:
   - Production boards with information like takt time, productivity rates, yields, on-time delivery rates
   - Safety indicators
   - Inventory reorder points
   - Walk paths
   - Visual work instructions
   - Employee skill boards
   - 5S status
   - Defects, e.g., non-conforming materials

Core Tool / Control Charts

What is it?

Control Charts are similar to Run Charts. The team, in addition to plotting data over time, calculates statistical control limits and places them on the Control Chart to assess whether the process is operating in a state of statistical control. If a process is considered in control, it is stable and predictable.

Why do it?

Control Charts are used to improve processes by identifying special cause variation. Special causes (also called assignable causes) are factors that can be detected and determined to be contributing to the change in the characteristic being charted.

Common cause variation (also called random chance) generally comes from all the many factors contributing a small amount of change in the variable or item of interest.

Processes exhibiting only common cause variation are said to be operating in a state of statistical control. Control Charts can be used to monitor processes over time for ongoing control.

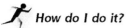

🏃 How do I do it?

1. Determine what variable or item needs to be charted.

- Given $Y = f(x)$, it is better, when possible, to control critical inputs (x's and X's) versus customer CTQs (critical to quality) to outputs. If the input, or some other leading indicator, can be controlled, it should be possible to achieve the desired output.

- Determine if the item to be charted represents data that is variable or discrete (attribute). If it is discrete data, will the defects or defectives be tracked? A defect is a single nonconformance. Items containing one or more defects could be considered not acceptable and deemed to be defective.

2. Determine the sampling plan. Consider:

- Data collection effort
- Cost
- Frequency of collection
- Sample size

Typical Sample Sizes for Control Charts

Control Chart	X̄ and S	X̄ and R	IMR	c Chart	u Chart	np Chart	p Chart
Sample Size	≥10	3 – 5	1	50 – 100	50 – 100	50 – 100	50 – 100

IMR = Individuals and Moving Range Chart

3. Determine which Control Chart to use.

Choosing the Control Chart

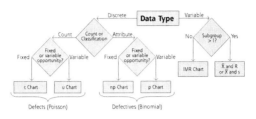

4. Begin data collection.
5. Calculate control limits.
   - See Appendix B for Control Chart formulas.
   - If creating a variable characteristic, see Appendix C for Control Chart constants based on your sample size.
   - Typically 20–25 subgroups (or data points if an Individuals and Moving Range Chart is being constructed) are used to calculate the control limits.
6. Interpret the Control Chart output. Use the typical rules described here to determine whether your process is out of control.

Rule 1: There is 1 point more than 3 standard deviations from the centerline. Process is out of control.

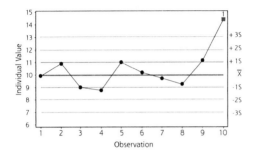

Rule 2: There are 9 consecutive points on the same side of the centerline. Process is out of control.

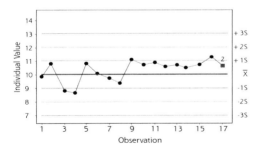

Rule 3: There are 6 consecutive points, all increasing or all decreasing. Process is out of control.

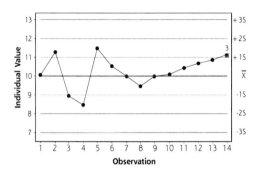

Rule 4: There are 14 consecutive points, alternating up and down. Process is out of control.

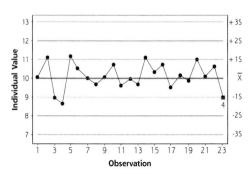

Rule 5: There are 2 out of 3 points more than 2 standard deviations from the same side of the centerline. Process is out of control.

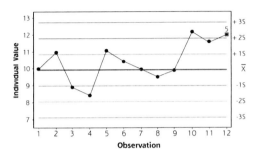

Rule 6: There are 4 out of 5 points more than 1 standard deviation from the same side of the centerline. Process is out of control.

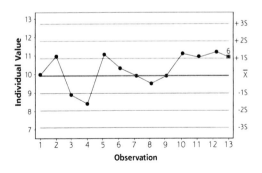

Rule 7: There are 15 consecutive points within 1 standard deviation of the centerline. Process is out of control.

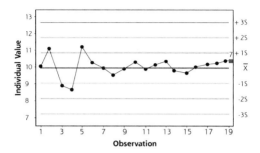

Rule 8: There are 8 consecutive points more than 1 standard deviation from the centerline. Process is out of control.

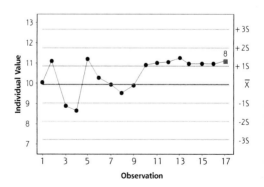

Note: The +/- 1 and +/- 2 sigma (standard deviation) limits are shown here for clarification of the rules. In practice, just the +/- 3 sigma limits are shown on a chart.

Tip: If your Control Charts match up with any of these rules, it is a signal that special cause variation is present. Your team's efforts should focus on identifying the source of the variation and potentially removing it.

Tip: Control limits represent the voice of the process (VOP), as they are calculated from the variation that exists in the process. Specification limits link back to customer requirements. While the process should be designed to meet customer specifications, the two limits are distinctly different and should not be confused.

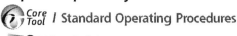

Step 3: Complete Project Documentation

Core Tool / Standard Operating Procedures

What is it?

A standard operating procedure describes the process of how work gets done. A standard operating procedure fits into an overall system of documentation.

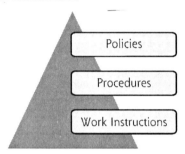

Policies: These are the general guiding directions set by management.

> **Example:** A bank may have a policy that any applicant must have three years of work experience before it will consider giving an applicant a loan.

Procedures: Describe who does what activity, and in what sequence. Activities are often displayed in a process map or flowchart.

Work instructions: Describe how to perform specific jobs and tasks that are required in the process.

> **Example:** A work instruction is created to explain how to perform a laboratory test. The instructions may be written or may be visual, with pictures, symbols, or colors.

Why do it?

Procedures and other levels of documentation are created to provide workers with a standardized approach to follow. Having a standardized approach tends to minimize human errors and defects.

🏃 How do I do it?

1. Determine what documentation currently exists.

2. Review what content needs to change.

3. Identify what level of the documentation needs to change: policy, procedure, work instruction, checklist, templates, etc.

4. Determine what format will best communicate the information: written, flowchart, visual aid, videotape, photograph or illustration, etc.

Tip: It is helpful to integrate much of the documentation using a visual management approach. Lengthy written procedures and work instructions tend not to be used consistently. Process maps can be used to shorten the documentation.

Tip: In the Measure phase, the current process is identified and documented. As the project progresses, controls and improvements are determined. The process of modifying the documentation should be done as appropriate.

Core Tool / Control Plan

What is it?

A control plan is a written summary of the system for managing a process. It lists the controls needed to ensure the proper output of the process. It does not, however, replace detailed process documentation like procedures or work instructions. A control plan, like the process map and FMEA chart, is a living document that should be transitioned to the process owners who can maintain the documentation over time as the process changes.

Why do it?

Control plans help people to prioritize resources on the required critical activities in a process. The structured approach helps people to minimize waste and improve quality. Control plans can also be used to aid in process troubleshooting, training, and process auditing.

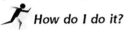

How do I do it?

1. Review current process documentation for the controls already identified.

2. Review project tools, e.g., process map, FMEA, to understand additional controls needed in the process.

3. Determine the control plan format to be used. Two formats are shown here: a traditional format, and a simplified format of a process management chart.

Typical information in a control plan includes:

- Process name and steps

- Approval dates

- Critical output and input variables to be controlled

- Specifications

- How the output and input variables are to be measured

- What sample size will be needed, and how frequently samples will be collected

- Who will measure and where

- The reaction plan if a problem develops

Traditional Control Plan Example

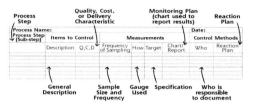

Process Management Chart Example

(Simplified Approach)

Process Flow	Indicators	Reaction Plan
Place Orders	Check five purchase orders per day for completeness. Verify signature and amount.	Contact manager of Purchasing and supplier.
Orders Received	Timeliness. Record on Individuals and Moving Range Chart.	Investigate cause.
Receiving Inspection	Accuracy of shipment. Utilize Check Sheet.	Contact manager of Receiving Inspection. Prepare for supplier a document listing nonconforming materials.

4. Determine how the control plan will be utilized by the work group.

5. Develop the control plan with the team.

6. Transition the responsibility of carrying out and maintaining the control plan to the process owner.

> **Tip:** Control plans can be the most important tool to implement. If a control plan is not implemented correctly, sustaining improvements may be difficult.

> **Tip:** Be sure to collaborate with the work team on the control plan. Without buy-in to the process controls and monitoring process, the control plan will not be used.

Core Tool / Audit Plan

What is it?

A Six Sigma audit plan is a plan to review the improved process at specified intervals to ensure that process controls remain in place and are adhered to so that the proper outputs of the process are maintained.

Why do it?

Organizations are dynamic. People change positions. Priorities are revised. If controls don't remain, then achieving the benefits of the project will be in jeopardy.

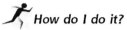 *How do I do it?*

1. Determine the critical items to be audited.

2. Develop the audit plan.

What is to be audited?

- Review the FMEA chart and the control plan for critical items.

Who will do the audit?

- It is common for the champion to be responsible for ensuring the audit plan is executed.

- A Green, Black, or Master Black Belt (or another independent individual) may be asked to perform the actual audit.

When will the audit be conducted?

- The frequency may depend on the criticality of the process, however, audits at 3, 6, and 12 months are useful.

Chapter **6**

Advanced Tools:
Green/Black-Belt Level

The following tools have been selected from the Green/Black-Belt-level tool kit. The intent is not that Yellow Belts should be able to create these tools, but for them to recognize the tools and to understand key aspects about them. The tools included in this section are: benchmarking, value stream maps, GR&R (Gauge Repeatability and Reproducibility), process capability, hypothesis testing, and design of experiments (DOE).

Benchmarking   Advanced DMAIC

🏃 What is it?

Benchmarking is a process of learning from others. Teams and organizations attempt to identify, study, and then replicate "best practices" for critical processes/areas of the business. Comparisons are typically measures in terms of quality, cost, or time. Ideally, benchmarking is done on a regular basis by the organization, not just in the Improve phase of a DMAIC project.

Why do it?

Benchmarking allows teams and organizations to understand organizational and process shortcomings and to inject new ideas into a process, based on what others are doing, and to develop an action plan to improve the organization's performance. Benchmarking is helpful to organizations in achieving breakthrough levels of improvement.

How do I do it?

1. Prepare for the study.

   - Understand customer needs.
   - Determine desired business outcomes.
   - Identify available resources and the budget.

2. Determine the type of study to be done.

   - **Internal.** Done with other areas or departments of the business. Limited opportunity may result.

   - **Competitive.** Focuses externally on current industry. May limit opportunity, depending on the industry.

   - **Functional.** Focuses on functional area, which are typically sources outside of the organization's industry.

   - **Collaborative.** When organizations come together to conduct benchmarking studies.

3. Identify a benchmarking partner or source.

4. Execute the study.

5. Analyze collected data.

6. Create an action plan based on the study. Adapt best practices for your project or organization.

> **Tip:** Benchmarking can be done with a partner company or through other resources such as: industry experts, trade publications, web sites, tours, former employees.

 Benchmarking partners may only want to participate with your request if they think they can learn something from you as well.

Value Stream Map Advanced DMAIC

✒ What is it?

A value stream map shows the communication, materials, and process flow of a process. Key information is included, like cycle times, the number of people in the process, value-added and non-value-added times, and changeover time. The value stream map is typically created in the Define or Measure phase of a project.

Why do it?

Value stream maps are often done when projects are aimed at reducing lead times, eliminating or reducing constraints, and/or improving flow. Value stream maps help teams to identify areas of opportunity by comparing the current state to a desired future state.

> *Tip:* Not every project will require a value stream map. Some projects may be best addressed with a process map. Some projects may require both maps.

How do I do it?

The Yellow Belt will most likely participate on a project team that will at some point need to do value stream mapping. However, Yellow Belts will not likely be responsible for creating the value stream map (VSM).

1. The team should prepare for the mapping activity. This could involve gathering data collection material, selecting the product or service in need of mapping, and scheduling access to the people and area of focus.

2. Create the current state VSM. The project leader (Master Black Belt, Black Belt, or Green Belt) will lead this activity.

Value Stream Map Example

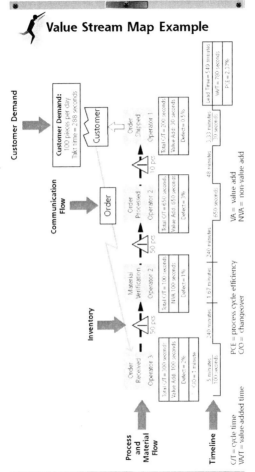

Customer Demand

Customer Demand:
100 pieces per day
Takt time = 288 seconds

Communication Flow

Order

Customer

Order Shipped

Inventory

50 pcs · 50 pcs · 10 pcs

Process and Material Flow

Order Received	Material Verification	Order Processed	Order Shipped
Operator 3	Operator 2	Operator 2	Operator 1
Total C/T = 300 seconds	Total C/T = 100 seconds	Total C/T = 650 seconds	Total C/T = 290 seconds
Value Add 100 seconds	NVA 100 seconds	Value Add 650 seconds	Value Add 30 seconds
Defect = 2%	Defect = 1%	Defect = 3%	Defect = 0.5%
C/O = 1 minute			

Lead Time = 549 minutes
VA/T = 780 seconds
PCE = 2.37%

Timeline

5 minutes · 240 minutes · 1.67 minutes · 240 minutes · 650 seconds · 48 minutes · 7.33 minutes
100 seconds · 30 seconds

C/T = cycle time
VA/T = value-added time

PCE = process cycle efficiency
C/O = changeover

VA = value add
NVA = non-value add

3. Analyze the current state map and create a future state VSM. The project leader (Master Black Belt, Black Belt, or Green Belt) will lead this activity.

4. Determine what specific project actions are needed to move from the current state VSM to the future state VSM.

See *The Lean Enterprise Memory Jogger*™, pages 15–28 for more detailed information on creating a value stream map.

Gauge Repeatability and Reproducibility (GR&R) Advanced DMAIC

GR&R for Variable Data

➤● *What is it?*

A variable GR&R allows a team to check if the measurement system is adequate for a continuous measurement. The repeatability and reproducibility of the measurement system is assessed.

Why do it?

A variable GR&R is done to make sure the measurement system variation is small compared to the total variation in the system.

Common GR&R Measures of Variation for Variable Data

	Acceptable	Excellent
% Contribution $= \dfrac{\hat{\sigma}^2 ms}{\hat{\sigma}^2 \text{ total}} \times 100$	< 9%	< 1%
% Precision to total variation $= \dfrac{\hat{\sigma} ms}{\hat{\sigma} \text{ total}} \times 100$	< 30%	< 10%
% Precision to tolerance $= \dfrac{6 \times \hat{\sigma} ms}{\text{tolerance}} \times 100$	< 30%	< 10%

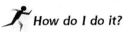 **How do I do it?**

The Yellow Belt will most likely participate on a project team that will at some point need to do a variable GR&R. However, Yellow Belts will not likely be responsible for conducting and analyzing the GR&R.

1. The team will identify the feature being measured that will be the focus of the study.

2. Identify the units and people that will be used in the study. Units that represent the full range of expected variation need to be identified. (Typically 5–10 units.) People that currently take the measurements should also be in the study.

3. Conduct the GR&R study and analyze the outcome. The project leader (Master Black Belt, Black Belt, or Green Belt) will lead this activity.

4. Make needed improvements to the measurement system.

See *The Black Belt Memory Jogger*™, pages 73–94 for information on how to conduct a GR&R study.

Gauge R&R (ANOVA) for Measure

Components of Variation

% P/TV = % precision to total variation
% P/T = % precision to tolerance

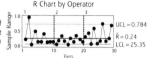

Stability of measurement system

R Chart by Operator

UCL = 0.784
R̄ = 0.24
LCL = 25.35

Control limits show measurement system error

X̄ Chart by Operator

UCL = 26.25
X̄ = 25.80
LCL = 25.35

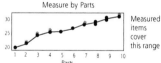

Measure by Parts

Measured items cover this range

Measure by Operator

Shows variation of measures by operator

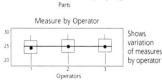

Interaction of Parts & Operator

© 2015 GOAL/QPC

GR&R for Attribute Data

🔷 What is it?

An attribute GR&R allows a team to check if the measurement system is adequate for measuring attribute data. The repeatability and reproducibility of the measurement system is assessed. Data could be attribute, nominal, or ordinal.

Attribute: good/bad, pass/fail, yes/no data

Nominal: labels like blue, green, red; or cracked, dented, scratched

Ordinal: high, medium, low; or 1st, 2nd, 3rd

Why do it?

An attribute GR&R is done if the data is discrete. It is done to make sure the measurement system variation is small compared to the total variation in the system.

Ideally, each appraiser's measurement would agree when repeated, and all appraisers' measures would match. In addition, all appraisers would agree with the standard, typically set by a subject matter expert.

A Kappa measure is sometimes used to assess how adequate the measurement system is.

< .7 System needs improvement

> .7 Good

> .9 Excellent

> **Tip:** A simpler approach for an attribute GR&R would be to just measure and report the percent agreement between the appraisers and the reference standard.

Attribute GR&R

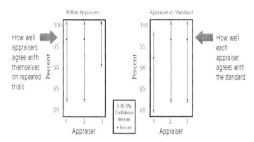

How well appraisers agree with themselves on repeated trials

How well each appraiser agrees with the standard

The standard can be an expert on the subject matter, a panel of individuals, or a customer.

How do I do it?

The Yellow Belt will most likely participate on a project team that will at some point need to do an attribute GR&R. However, Yellow Belts will not likely be responsible for conducting and analyzing the GR&R.

1. The team will identify the feature being measured that will be the focus of the study.

2. Identify the units and people that will be used in the study. Units that represent the full range of expected variation need to be identified.

(Typically 20–30 units.) People that currently take the measurements should also be in the study.

3. Conduct the GR&R study and analyze the outcome. The project leader (Master Black Belt, Black Belt, or Green Belt) will lead this activity.

4. Make needed improvements to the measurement system.

See *The Black Belt Memory Jogger™*, pages 73–94 for information on how to conduct a GR&R study.

Process Capability $\quad$ Advanced DMAIC

🏃 What is it?

Process capability is discussed in Chapter 2. Depending on the software being used, there are numerous ways the analysis could be presented. Included here is a common process capability output that the Yellow Belt may see in a project, and some additional capability metrics.

The Cp, Cpk, Pp, and Ppk metrics are commonly used in many organizations.

$$C_p = \frac{USL - LSL}{6\hat{\sigma}_{ST}}$$

$$C_{pk} = Min.\left[\frac{USL - \bar{X}}{3\hat{\sigma}_{ST}} \text{ or } \frac{\bar{X} - LSL}{3\hat{\sigma}_{ST}}\right]$$

$$P_p = \frac{USL - LSL}{6\hat{\sigma}_{LT}}$$

$$P_{pk} = Min.\left[\frac{USL - \bar{X}}{3\hat{\sigma}_{LT}} \text{ or } \frac{\bar{X} - LSL}{3\hat{\sigma}_{LT}}\right]$$

Cp and Cpk represent the short-term capability. Cp is the ratio of the specification range divided by the natural variation of the process. It is an estimate of the process entitlement (how good the process could be without significant investment).

Cpk takes into consideration the centering of the process and is the metric that is often tracked by organizations. Pp and Ppk represent what happens to capability over the longer term.

Cpk	Interpretation
<1.00	Not Capable
1.00-1.33	Marginally Capable
>1.33	Capable

Process Capability Example

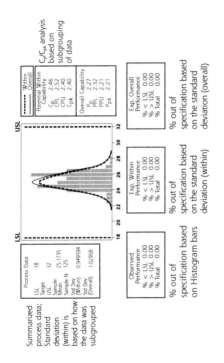

Summarized process data; Standard deviation (within) is based on how the data was subgrouped

Process Data

LSL	18
Target	*
USL	32
Sample Mean	25.1735
Sample N	125
StDev (Within)	0.949594
StDev (Overall)	1.02958

C_p/C_{pk} analysis based on subgrouping of data

----- Within
——— Overall

Potential (Within) Capability	
C_p	2.46
CPL	2.52
CPU	2.40
C_{pk}	2.40

Overall Capability	
P_p	2.27
PPL	2.32
PPU	2.21
P_{pk}	2.21

Observed Performance

% < LSL	0.00
% > USL	0.00
% Total	0.00

% out of specification based on Histogram bars

Exp. Within Performance

% < LSL	0.00
% > USL	0.00
% Total	0.00

% out of specification based on the standard deviation (within)

Exp. Overall Performance

% < LSL	0.00
% > USL	0.00
% Total	0.00

% out of specification based on the standard deviation (overall)

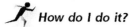

🏃 *How do I do it?*

Typically these steps are followed:

1. Check for data normality.

2. If not normal, check for factors to stratify the data by:

   - Time
   - Input factors

3. If stratification is not successful, look for an alternative distribution to use, e.g., log-normal, Weibull.

4. If no alternative distribution fits the data, then consider transformation of the data.

   - Box Cox transformation
   - Johnson transformation

Hypothesis Testing

What is it?

Sample statistics are used to test if populations are statistically different from one another. Tested statistics could be averages, standard deviations, or proportions and rates. Some common hypothesis tests are:

Test Selection Matrix	Continuous Y	Discrete Y
Continuous X	Regression	Logistic Regression
Discrete X	t-Test ANOVA	Chi-Square Test Proportion

Why do it?

Often decisions need to be made to determine if statistical differences are present without the benefit of all of the data available. In hypothesis testing, two types of risk exist: alpha and beta risk.

Alpha risk: The probability of finding a statistical difference when one does not exist (a false positive). Typically .05 is used.

Beta risk: The probability of not finding a statistical difference when one does exist (a false negative). Typically .10 is used.

The "power of the test" is related to the Beta risk. It is the probability of finding the statistical difference when one exists. In other words, 1 − the Beta risk is equal to the "power of the test."

How do I do it?

The Yellow Belt will most likely participate on a project team that will at some point need to do hypothesis testing. However, Yellow Belts will not likely be responsible for doing the data analysis.

$$H_0: \mu_a = \mu_b$$
$$H_0: \sigma^2_a = \sigma^2_b$$

If the null hypothesis is rejected, the alternative hypothesis is selected. The corresponding alternative hypothesis statement would be:

$$H_a: \mu_a \neq \mu_b$$
$$H_a: \sigma^2_a \neq \sigma^2_b$$

Example: A Black Belt tested the output from two suppliers to see if the average output was the same. A two-sample T-test was run. The team was presented with the following analysis:

Hypothesis Testing Example

Two-sample T-test for Supplier 1 vs. Supplier 2

	N	Mean	StDev	SE Mean
Supplier 1	20	520	114	25
Supplier 2	20	509.9	31.8	7.1

Difference = mu (Supplier 1) − mu (Supplier 2)
Estimate for difference: 10.2
95% CI for difference: (-44.6, 65.1)
T-test of difference = 0 (vs. not =):
T-Value = 0.39
P-Value = 0.702
DF = 21

Since the p-value > Alpha (0.5), it is assumed the samples are the same (fail to reject the H_o).

See *The Black Belt Memory Jogger*™, pages 149–156 for general information on hypothesis testing; pages 170–178 for information on conducting a regression study; and pages 179–184 for information on conducting a logistic regression study.

Design of Experiments (DOE) Advanced DMAIC

🏊 What is it?

Design of Experiments (DOE) is a family of statistical techniques that helps teams actively collect and analyze data to understand the effects of changing input factors on one or more responses. A DOE would involve testing combinations of the input factors in order to find the desired level of the output. DOE's typically fall into one of three categories: Screening, Characterization, and Optimization.

Why do it?

It may be unclear when analyzing historical data what factors were changing. As a result, determining the relationship between the input and output may be difficult. A DOE allows the experimenter to determine the true cause and effect relationship between the variables, including factor interactions.

DOE Type	DOE Design
Screening	Fractional Factorial Design
Characterization	Full Factorial Design
Optimization	Response Surface Design

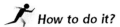

How to do it?

The Yellow Belt will most likely participate on a project team that will at some point need to do a designed experiment. However, Yellow Belts will not likely be responsible for setting up or analyzing the designed experiment.

For efficiency, the experimenter will typically start with two levels per factor. The steps for data analysis will be:

1. Collect data per DOE matrix.

2. Conduct graphical analysis.

3. Do the appropriate statistical test.

4. Reduce the model as needed. (Take out non-significant terms.)

5. Check model adequacy (residual analysis).

Example of a Full-Factorial Experiment
(3 factors, 2 levels)

Std Order	Run Order	Center Pt	Blocks	Factor A	Factor B	Factor C	Response
1	1	1	1	-1	-1	-1	Response 1
2	2	1	1	+1	-1	-1	Response 2
3	3	1	1	-1	+1	-1	Response 3
4	4	1	1	+1	+1	-1	Response 4
5	5	1	1	-1	-1	+1	Response 5
6	6	1	1	+1	-1	+1	Response 6
7	7	1	1	-1	+1	+1	Response 7
8	8	1	1	+1	+1	+1	Response 8

Note: -1 is the factor's low level and +1 is its high level.

See *The Black Belt Memory Jogger*™, 185–210, for information on fractional and full-factorial designs, and response surface designs.

Acronyms

5S	sort, straighten, shine, standardize, sustain
6M's	people (man), machines, materials, methods, measurements, and environment (Mother Nature)
6σ	Six Sigma
ANOVA	analysis of variance
CTQ	critical to quality
DFSS	design for Six Sigma
DMADV	define, measure, analyze, design, verify
DMAIC	define, measure, analyze, improve, control
DOE	design of experiments
DPMO	defects per million opportunities
DPO	defects per opportunity
DPU	defects per unit
FMEA	failure mode and effects analysis
GR&R	gauge (or gage) repeatability and reproducibility
KPI	key performance indicator
LSS	Lean Six Sigma
MSA	measurement systems analysis
PPM	parts per million defective
QFD	quality function deployment
ROI	return on investment
SIPOC	suppliers, inputs, process, outputs, customers
SOP	standard operating procedures
SPC	statistical process control
VOB	voice of the business
VOC	voice of the customer
VOP	voice of the process
WIP	work in process (or progress)

Glossary

As a Yellow Belt, it will be helpful to understand various terms discussed during a Lean Six Sigma project. This glossary lists many commonly used terms and their meaning. Numbers are spelled and listed alphabetically.

Action plan: A specific plan to achieve objectives identified during an improvement project. Example: Unfinished tasks from a kaizen event. Any project plan covers what is to be done, who is to be responsible, and when the due dates are.

Affinity Diagram: One of the seven management and planning tools used to organize information into categories. (The information is usually gathered during a brainstorming activity.)

Alpha risk: The maximum level of risk considered acceptable when rejecting a true null hypothesis during a hypothesis test. Typically set at .05.

Analysis of variance (ANOVA): A statistical technique for understanding if mean differences are present in a data set containing a continuous output and one or more discrete inputs. It breaks down the total variation of a data set into the variation due to the factor(s) and the error.

Anderson-Darling test for normality: When the P-value is <0.05, we conclude the data comes from a non-normal population, and when the P-value >0.05, we conclude the data comes from a normal population.

Assignable cause: A source of variation which is non-random in nature and causes instability in the process. An assignable cause is signaled by data points outside the control limits and/or non- random patterns within the control limits. Also called "special cause" variation.

Attribute data: Good/bad, pass/fail go/no-go information. Discrete data with only two outcomes, and is typically modeled with the binomial distribution.

Audit plan: After the project is concluded, audits are conducted to ensure improvements are maintained. The plan should include: What is to be audited? Who will do the audit? and When will the audit be conducted?

Batch production: A technique for mass production where items are built and transferred from one step to the next in batches.

Benchmarking: A structured methodology used to compare a company's system/process performance against another entity. It is often done against that of "best in class" companies, although it can be limited to comparisons within an industry or the company itself.

Best practice: A superior method or practice usually recognized as "best" within the organization or by other peer organizations.

Beta risk: The probability of failing to reject the null hypothesis when, in reality, it is false. 1 – beta risk = the power of the test. Typically set at .10.

Box plot: Also called a Box and Whisker plot. A box plot summarizes a set of variable data into five values: the highest value, the upper quartile, the median, the lower quartile, and the lowest value.

Black Belt: A full-time Six Sigma team leader who is responsible for implementing DMAIC process improvement projects.

© 2015 GOAL/QPC

Brainstorming: A technique used to generate a quantity of ideas on a particular topic. Each person is asked to think creatively and write down as many ideas as possible. Ideas are not discussed or reviewed until after the brainstorming session. There are a number of variations of brainstorming.

Business-value added: A term that describes a process step or activity that is not required for the achievement of the process output for the customer, but is needed by the business.

Capability analysis: The statistical comparison of the actual performance of a process with its specification limits. Typical measures include: Cp, Cpk, Pp, Ppk, defects per unit (DPU), defects per million opportunities (DPMO), percent (%) conformance and nonconformance.

Cause & Effect Diagram: One of the seven basic tools of quality used for documenting and analyzing inputs that cause process variation. Also referred to as the Ishikawa Diagram or a Fishbone Diagram. A variation of the 6 M's—Materials, Machines, Methods, Man (people), Measurement, and Mother Nature (the environment)—is often used as the major headings in the diagram.

Champion: A Six Sigma champion is typically a business leader/senior manager who addresses Six Sigma-related organizational issues, identifies projects, and ensures that project resources are available. Champions guide the project on business issues and participate in project tollgate reviews. In larger organizations the responsibilities might be broken into deployment champions and project champions. Typically, each area of the business or product or plant has a champion.

Change management: The process of bringing planned change to an organization. A change management process usually involves communication and orchestrated activities to understand the barriers to the introduction of change.

Charter: A document written by management that transfers authority for process improvement to an improvement team. Charters typically contain a problem statement, the business case, goals, the project scope, milestones, and the needed team resources.

Checklist: Checklists contain the key information needed to assess if an activity was done correctly. Checklists are mistake-proofing tools that can be very effective in transactional processes.

Check Sheet: One of the seven basic tools of quality, check sheets are a simple data recording tool. The check sheet is custom designed by the user, which allows for quick data entry and interpretation of the results.

Common causes: All the small sources of variation that are inherent in every process when no assignable causes of variation are present. If only common cause variation is present, a process should be stable and predictable and can often be modeled by a normal distribution. It is also called "random cause" variation.

Continuous data: Data that can be subdivided to less than a whole unit. Examples: temperature (75.2 degrees), length (8.75 inches), weight (225.8 pounds). Also referred to as variable data.

Control: A process state in which all special causes of variation have been removed. Processes can be monitored, usually by means of a Control Chart, to determine if they are in control. In-control processes are also referred to as being stable and predictable.

Control Chart: A characteristic of interest is plotted on a chart containing statistically developed upper and lower control limits, and a centerline. The intent of a Control Chart is to determine if a process is stable, predictable, and free of assignable causes of variation.

Control limits: The natural boundaries of a process are typically measured as $\pm 3\sigma$. Control Charts use these values as the upper control limit (UCL) and the lower control limit (LCL).

Control plan: A document that summarizes the required characteristics for the quality of a product or service. Typically it includes: process identification information, approvals, measures, specifications, sampling frequency, control methods, and a reaction plan.

Correlation: A measure of the relationship between two data sets of continuous data variables. The correlation coefficient ranges from -1 to +1. As the value gets closer to -1 or +1, there is a stronger relationship. Correlation does not imply causation.

Cost of poor quality (COPQ): Also referred to as Cost of Quality (COQ). Typically is measured in terms of four cost components: prevention costs, appraisal costs, internal failure costs, and external failure costs.

Critical to quality (CTQ): A critical-to-quality item is one that has an impact on a customer's view of quality and determines the customer's level of satisfaction.

Cycle time: The elapsed time between the start and completion of a task or an entire process, e.g., the time between receipt and delivery of an order.

Defect: A defect is a condition that results in an "unfitness" of use or nonconformance against a specification. One or more defects could make an item defective.

Defective: An item containing one or more defects of the quality characteristic being evaluated.

Discrete data: Data that can't be broken down to less than a whole unit. Examples: the number of defective parts in a sample, the number of defects on a part, or pass/fail data. Pass/fail (yes/no, 0/1) data is often considered a subset of discrete data and is referred to as attribute data.

Design of experiments (DOE): A DOE is a test or series of tests where the inputs are changed per a structured plan in order to understand the inputs' effect on the output.

DFSS (Design for Six Sigma): A systematic methodology utilizing tools, training, and measurements to ensure that the quality levels of a product or process meet customer expectations. A number of models are used to do this. Two common models are DMADV and IDOV.

DMADV: A commonly used DFSS model consisting of five phases: Define, Measure, Analyze, Design, and Verify.

DMAIC: A commonly used five-phase, process-improvement model consisting of: Define, Measure, Analyze, Improve, and Control. Six Sigma and Lean Six Sigma projects follow this methodology.

DPMO (defects per million opportunities): The actual number of defects occurring divided by the total number of opportunities for a defect and multiplied by one million.

DPO (defects per opportunity): The actual number of defects occurring divided by the total number of opportunities for a defect.

DPU: Defects per unit is calculated by dividing the total number of defects by the number of units.

Eight wastes: 1. Transportation, 2. Inventory, 3. Motion, 4. Waiting, 5. Overproduction, 6. Overprocessing, 7. Defects, and 8. Underutilized people. Used to help identify areas of non- value-add for the customer.

Entitlement: As good as a process can get without capital investment. The goal in a DMAIC project is to close the gap between current performance and entitlement.

Error: Errors cause defects to occur. Errors typically originate from the 6 M's, which are: Materials, Machines, Methods, Man (people), Measurement, and Mother Nature (the environment).

Failure Mode and Effects Analysis (FMEA): A structured methodology to identify potential failure modes, effects, and causes in a process. Risk is measured via a Risk Priority Number (RPN). Issue resolution and RPN reduction is also tracked.

Five S's: Five terms beginning with "S" (based on the original Japanese words Sort, Store, Shine, Standardize, and Sustain) that are utilized to create a workplace suited for standard work and visual control. Sort is to separate out unneeded materials and remove them from the work area. Store is to put everything in its place. Shine is to conduct an area cleanup. Standardize is to standardize the approach of Sort, Store, and Shine. Sustain is to create the habit of following the first four S's.

Five Whys (also 5 Whys): A simple technique for discovering the root causes of a problem and showing the relationship of causes by repeatedly asking "Why?" Usually it is enough to take the questioning to a fifth level, hence "five whys."

Flowchart: A graphical depiction of the steps in a process. A flowchart shows all the steps in a process and the sequence of the steps by means of connecting lines with arrows showing the process flow.

Gauge Repeatability & Reproducibility (GR&R): The evaluation process of determining if a measurement system is adequate by understanding if measurements taken with it are repeatable and reproducible. GR&R is one tool in the measurement-systems-analysis toolkit. Gage is another spelling.

Green Belt: A part-time Six Sigma team leader who is responsible for implementing improvements in his or her area of the organization.

Histogram: One of the seven basic tools of quality, a Histogram is a graphical summary of a set of data showing the frequency of values obtained for defined bin ranges.

Hypothesis testing: Statistically determining whether two or more populations differ significantly. A null hypothesis is constructed that assumes no significant difference and is ultimately rejected or is failed to be rejected. If the null hypothesis is rejected, the alternative hypothesis is assumed to be true.

IDOV: A commonly used DFSS model consisting of Identify, Design, Optimize, and Verify.

Inputs: The workers, tools, materials, and procedures used in a process to produce the output(s) delivered to customers.

IPO Map: See Process map.

Kaizen: A Japanese term that means "gradual unending improvement by doing little things better" to set and achieve increasingly higher standards.

Key Performance Indicator (KPI): A statistical measure of how well an organization is doing. A KPI may measure a company's financial, quality-related or employee-related performance.

Lean manufacturing: An initiative focused on identifying value to the customer, determining the value stream, creating process flow, allowing material to advance at the pull of the customer, and ultimately allowing the organization to seek perfection.

Lean Six Sigma: A structured process-improvement methodology that provides businesses with the tools to improve the capability of their business processes. Lean Six Sigma blends both Lean and Six Sigma tools and follows the DMAIC project structure.

Master Black Belt: Full-time Six Sigma practitioners responsible for training, leading larger projects, project coaching, and assisting the different champions in the company with selecting projects.

Mean: A measure of central tendency; the arithmetic average of all measurements in a data set.

Measurement system: The measurement system includes the actual gauge, method, environmental conditions, and appraisers.

Measurement system analysis (MSA): The MSA toolkit includes several studies that are designed to evaluate the measurement system. They include: stability studies, gauge R&R studies, bias studies, and linearity studies.

Median: The middle number or center value of a set of data in which all the data are arranged in sequence.

Milestones: Events that signify progress in the project. In a Six Sigma/Lean Six Sigma project, milestones are typically defined as the completion of each of the DMAIC phases.

Mode: The value occurring most frequently in a data set.

Muda: Japanese word for waste. Muda is an activity that consumes resources but creates no value for the customer.

Noise: Inputs that cause random and expected process variation. Noise factors are usually not controlled or not considered feasible to control.

Non-value added: A term that describes a process step or activity that is not required for the achievement of the process output. A non-value-added item is identified and considered for potential elimination.

Normal distribution: A distribution can be thought of as a model that describes a set of data. A normal distribution is important because it can be used to model data from many situations. It is used for continuous data and is symmetrical around the average of the data set.

Normality: A normality test is a statistical process used to determine if a sample of data fits a normal distribution. A normality test can be performed mathematically, e.g., an Anderson- Darling test for normality, or graphically via a probability plot.

Outputs: The intended result of a process such as: products, materials, services or information provided to customers (internal or external), or unintended results such as waste and defects from a process.

Overprocessing: One of the eight wastes. It describes a situation where the product or service has taken more steps to produce than what is required by the customer.

Overproduction: One of the eight wastes. It describes a situation where more is produced than what is required by the customer, or where it is produced sooner than what the customer requires.

Pareto Chart: One of the seven basic tools of quality, Pareto Charts are a graphical tool for ranking causes from most significant to least significant. Frequency or cost could be used for the ranking. Joseph Juran generalized the original concept developed by 19th century economist Vilfredo Pareto. The Pareto principle suggests most effects come from relatively few causes, that is, 80% of the effects come from 20% of the possible causes.

Parts per million defective (PPM): The actual number of defective parts found in a sample divided by the total number of parts in the sample and then multiplied by one million.

PICK Chart: An L-shaped matrix that helps a team to prioritize projects by comparing the project payoff versus its ease of implementation. The acronym PICK stands for: Possible, Implement, Challenge, and Kill.

Population: The complete set of items from which a sample can be drawn. In process improvement activity, the population is rarely known. Sample statistics are used to estimate parameters of a population.

Process map: A block diagram depicting the steps in a process, with inputs and outputs identified for each step. In Six Sigma, this is often referred to as an IPO map.

Process owner: The person responsible for coordinating the work functions and activities of a process. The process owner has the authority to make changes in the process as required and manages the entire process cycle to ensure performance effectiveness.

Progress reviews: A progress review occurs between each phase of a Six Sigma project to ensure that the intent of the project is maintained. Reviews are attended by key individuals: the champion, the Master Black Belt, Black Belts, Green Belts, and key stakeholders. It is more commonly called a tollgate review.

Project scope: The defined boundaries of a project defined in the Charter. The scope includes work content established by starting and ending points and project duration.

Quality Function Deployment (QFD): A structured methodology for translating customer needs into design targets. The starting input into the QFD is the voice of the customer (VOC).

Range: One measure of dispersion in a data set. The range is the difference between the highest and lowest value.

Regression analysis: A statistical technique for determining the functional relationship between one continuous response and one or more independent continuous variables.

Run Chart: A chart which displays variable data in sequence over time so trends can be understood.

Sample: A subset of the overall population.

Scatter Diagram: One of the seven basic tools of quality, Scatter Diagrams are a graphical technique to analyze the relationship between two continuous variables.

Sigma: A term for standard deviation taken from the Greek letter σ, used in statistics as a measure of variation around the mean. A smaller value implies items in the group are more consistent than if a larger value is obtained.

Sigma level: For a process with a unilateral specification, the sigma level is the number of standard deviations between the average and the specification limit. For a bilateral specification, the total probability of a defect is put into the right tail of the curve and the sigma level would be the number of standard deviations between the average and the ordinate that corresponds to the area for the total probability of a defect.

SIPOC Diagram: Often done in advance of a more detailed process map, a SIPOC Diagram is a tool for defining business processes by listing Suppliers, Inputs, Process, Outputs, and Customers. Requirements of the customers and the "process trigger," (e.g., a customer places an order, a MRP system generates a work order), may also be included.

Six M's: Man (Personnel), Machines (Equipment), Methods, Materials, Measurements, and Mother Nature (Environment). The Six M's are useful in helping to organize potential causes of a defect (or defects) in a Cause & Effect Diagram.

Six Sigma: A structured process improvement methodology that provides businesses with the tools to improve the capability of their business processes. A process can be said to have a Six Sigma level of performance if there are six standard deviations between the process target and the specification limits. Per the original definition, Six Sigma equals 3.4 defects per million opportunities (DPMO).

Solution Selection Matrix: An L-shaped matrix used to prioritize potential solutions. It compares potential solutions to how important certain criteria are to the customer.

Stakeholder: Any individual, group, or organization that will have a significant impact on, or will be significantly impacted by the quality of the product or service an organization provides. A stakeholder analysis is often done early in a project to ensure the stakeholder needs are understood.

Standard deviation: A calculated measure of variation, indicating the spread of the data set around the mean. Also see Sigma.

Standard work: A concise description of work activity in a process specifying cycle time, takt time, work sequence of specific tasks, and the minimum inventory of parts on hand needed to conduct the activity.

Statistical Process Control (SPC): The application of statistical techniques to control a process through the use of Control Charts.

Takt time: Takt time is the heartbeat of the process. Takt time is calculated by dividing the available production time by the customer demand in some given time frame. The goal is to have process cycle times close to the takt time without going over.

Tollgate review: A tollgate review occurs between each phase of a Six Sigma project to ensure that the intent of the project is maintained. Reviews are attended by key individuals: the champion, the Master Black Belt, Black Belts, Green Belts, and key stakeholders.

Value added: A term that describes a process step or activity that is required for the achievement of the process output. In order to be value added, a step or activity needs to be something the customer is willing to pay for, transforms the product or service, and is done right the first time.

Value stream: All activities, both value added and non-value added, required to bring a product or service from an initial state to a completed state as defined by the customer. The value stream would include the communication flow, process flow, and material flow.

Value stream map: A value stream map shows the communication, materials, and process flow of a process. Key information is included: cycle times, the number of people in the process, value-added time, non-value-added time, and changeover time.

Variance: The standard deviation squared. Many formulas require the use of the variance (instead of the standard deviation) due to its property of being additive.

Variable data: See Continuous data.

Visual management: Visual management is a set of visual techniques that help teams to see the status of production, visual controls, standards, and performance indicators.

Voice of the business (VOB): The VOB is derived from the financial, strategic, or tactical needs of the business. Perceived deficiencies are often the reasons behind the launch of a Lean Six Sigma/Six Sigma project.

Voice of the customer (VOC): The stated and unstated requirements and expectations of customers relative to products or services. Capturing and analyzing the voice of the customer is often a starting point for many projects. VOC is most effective when captured on an ongoing basis.

Voice of the process (VOP): The VOP describes what the process is achieving. What is its process variation? What is the process average? Is it stable and in control?

---

y = f (x): The transfer function that describes how the process output is related to the process inputs, where y is equal to the outputs and x is equal to the inputs. Process outputs (y's) are a function of the critical process inputs (x's). This could be expressed as a regression formula or a list of the critical x's.

Yellow Belt: A Lean Six Sigma/Six Sigma team member who has received the appropriate level of training to support a Green/Black Belt in a DMAIC project.

Yield: The proportion or percentage of the process output that conforms to customer specifications.

Z score: A value that corresponds to a specific proportion (area under the curve) from a standard normal distribution. It represents the number of standard deviations from the mean to some value of interest, which is typically a specification limit. If a process has a unilateral specification limit, the z score would equal the sigma level.

Appendix A:
Sigma Level to Yield Conversion

Sigma Level $_{ST}$	DPMO $_{LT}$	Yield $_{LT}$
6.0	3.4	99.99966%
5.9	5.4	99.99946%
5.8	8.5	99.99915%
5.7	13	99.99867%
5.6	21	99.99793%
5.5	32	99.99683%
5.4	48	99.99519%
5.3	72	99.99277%
5.2	108	99.98922%
5.1	159	99.98409%
5.0	233	99.97674%
4.9	337	99.9663%
4.8	483	99.9517%
4.7	687	99.9313%
4.6	968	99.9032%
4.5	1,350	99.8650%
4.4	1,866	99.8134%
4.3	2,555	99.7445%
4.2	3,467	99.6533%
4.1	4,661	99.5339%
4.0	6,210	99.3790%
3.9	8,198	99.180%
3.8	10,724	98.928%
3.7	13,903	98.610%
3.6	17,864	98.214%
3.5	22,750	97.725%
3.4	28,717	97.128%
3.3	35,930	96.407%
3.2	44,565	95.543%
3.1	54,799	94.520%
3.0	66,807	93.319%

ST = Short Term, LT = Long Term, DPMO = defects per million opportunities

Sigma Level to Yield Conversion

Sigma Level $_{ST}$	DPMO $_{LT}$	Yield $_{LT}$
2.9	80,757	91.92%
2.8	96,800	90.32%
2.7	115,070	88.49%
2.6	135,666	86.43%
2.5	158,655	84.13%
2.4	184,060	81.59%
2.3	211,855	78.81%
2.2	241,964	75.80%
2.1	274,253	72.57%
2.0	308,538	69.15%
1.9	344,578	65.5%
1.8	382,089	61.8%
1.7	420,740	57.9%
1.6	460,172	54.0%
1.5	500,000	50.0%
1.4	539,828	46.0%
1.3	579,260	42.1%
1.2	617,911	38.2%
1.1	655,422	34.5%
1.0	691,462	30.9%
0.9	725,747	27.4%
0.8	758,036	24.2%
0.7	788,145	21.2%
0.6	815,940	18.4%
0.5	841,345	15.9%
0.4	864,334	13.6%
0.3	884,930	11.5%
0.2	903,200	9.7%
0.1	919,243	8.1%
0.0	933,193	6.7%

ST = Short Term, LT = Long Term, DPMO = defects per million opportunities

Appendix B:
Control Chart Limits

Control Chart	Control Limits	
p Chart (Fraction Defective)	$\bar{p} \pm 3\sqrt{\dfrac{\bar{p}(1-\bar{p})}{n}}$	
np Chart (Number Defective)	$n\bar{p} \pm 3\sqrt{n\bar{p}(1-\bar{p})}$	
u Chart (Defect Per Unit)	$\bar{u} \pm 3\sqrt{\dfrac{\bar{u}}{n}}$	
c Chart (Number of Defects)	$\bar{c} \pm 3\sqrt{\bar{c}}$	
$\bar{X}$ and s Chart	$\bar{X}$ Chart	$\bar{\bar{X}} \pm A_3\bar{s}$
	s Chart	$UCL_s = B_4\bar{s}$ $LCL_s = B_3\bar{s}$
$\bar{X}$ and R Chart	$\bar{X}$ Chart	$\bar{\bar{X}} \pm A_2\bar{R}$
	R Chart	$UCL_R = D_4\bar{R}$ $LCL_R = D_3\bar{R}$
Individuals and Moving Range	X Chart	$\bar{X} \pm E_2\bar{R}_m$
	R_m Chart	$UCL_{Rm} = D_4\bar{R}_m$ $LCL_{Rm} = D_3\bar{R}_m$

Appendix C:
Control Chart Constants

Sample Size	$\bar{X}$ and R Chart			$\bar{X}$ and s Chart			IMR Chart			
	A_2	D_3	D_4	A_3	B_3	B_4	E_2	D_3	D_4	d_2
2	1.88	0	3.267	2.659	0	3.267	2.659	0	3.267	1.128
3	1.023	0	2.574	1.954	0	2.568	1.772	0	2.574	1.693
4	0.729	0	2.282	1.628	0	2.266	1.457	0	2.282	2.059
5	0.577	0	2.114	1.427	0	2.089	1.29	0	2.114	2.326
6	0.483	0	2.004	1.287	0.03	1.97	1.184	0	2.004	2.534
7	0.419	0.076	1.924	1.182	0.118	1.882	1.109	0.076	1.924	2.704
8	0.373	0.136	1.864	1.099	0.185	1.815	1.054	0.136	1.864	2.847
9	0.337	0.184	1.816	1.032	0.239	1.761	1.01	0.184	1.816	2.97
10	0.308	0.223	1.777	0.975	0.284	1.716	0.975	0.223	1.777	3.078

IMR Chart = Individuals and Moving Range Chart

Index

Y

Z